Wag the Dog

Wag the Dog: A Study on Film and Reality in the Digital Age

Eleftheria Thanouli

Bloomsbury Academic
An imprint of Bloomsbury Publishing Inc

B L O O M S B U R Y
NEW YORK • LONDON • NEW DELHI • SYDNEY

Bloomsbury Academic
An imprint of Bloomsbury Publishing Inc

1385 Broadway	50 Bedford Square
New York	London
NY 10018	WC1B 3DP
USA	UK

www.bloomsbury.com

BLOOMSBURY and the Diana logo are trademarks of Bloomsbury Publishing Plc

First published 2013
First published in paperback 2015

© Eleftheria Thanouli, 2013, 2015

All rights reserved. No part of this publication may be reproduced or transmitted in any form or by any means, electronic or mechanical, including photocopying, recording, or any information storage or retrieval system, without prior permission in writing from the publishers.

No responsibility for loss caused to any individual or organization acting on or refraining from action as a result of the material in this publication can be accepted by Bloomsbury or the author.

Library of Congress Cataloging-in-Publication Data
Thanouli, Eleftheria.
Wag the dog : a study on film and reality in the digital age / by Eleftheria Thanouli.
pages cm
Includes bibliographical references and index.
ISBN 978-1-4411-8936-3 (hardback) – ISBN 978-1-4411-2281-0 (e-pub) – ISBN 978-1-4411-9871-6 (e-pdf) 1. Wag the dog (Motion picture) 2. Motion pictures–Philosophy. 3. Motion pictures–Social aspects–United States. I. Title.
PN1997.W25T47 2013
791.43'72–dc23
2013020883

ISBN: HB: 978-1-4411-8936-3
PB: 978-1-5013-0727-0
ePub: 978-1-4411-2281-0
ePDF: 978-1-4411-9871-6

Typeset by Fakenham Prepress Solutions, Fakenham, Norfolk NR21 8NN

To Yannis Tzioumakis

Contents

Acknowledgements viii
Introduction 1

1   *Wag the Dog* and Narrative Analysis   15
2   *Wag the Dog* and the Digital   49
3   *Wag the Dog* and the Media   77
4   *Wag the Dog* and Politics in Hollywood   105

Conclusion: *Wag the Dog* and its Universe   143
Bibliography   153
Index   163

Acknowledgements

My interest in *Wag the Dog* goes back to my undergraduate studies in Journalism and Mass Media. At the time, it was my professor Grigoris Paschalidis who drew my attention to Levinson's film and I am truly grateful for that. My special thanks goes to Yannis Tzioumakis who encouraged me to write a monograph on *Wag the Dog*, and to Katie Gallof who helped me accommodate in this monograph a wide range of ideas and issues. Thomas Elsaesser also offered, as usual, his valuable comments and support in the early stages of my writing. I am indebted to Giannis Kolaxizis and Sotiris Petridis for their technical assistance. Finally, I would like to thank my friends and family for their patience and support. My husband Achilleas and my daughter Anastasia have been an inexhaustible source of inspiration and love.

Introduction

Life imitates Art far more than Art imitates Life
Oscar Wilde, *The Decay of Lying*[1]

Wag the Dog is a good example to test Oscar Wilde's claim. Directed by Barry Levinson and released in the theatres a few weeks before the outbreak of the Monica Lewinsky scandal in the press, the film appeared to prove the Irish wit right. The real life occurrences, namely President Clinton's sexual affair with a White House intern and his subsequent attacks against foreign distant targets, seemed outright inspired by the movie plot. Yet, things are not quite that simple. In fact, this entire monograph is dedicated to exploring the complex relation between art and life, or rather cinema and reality, in order to do justice to the fine nuances of their intrinsic ties. These ties have occupied critics and scholars ever since the cinematic medium made its first steps in the beginning of the twentieth century. The result was a number of theoretical observations and philosophical positions regarding the ways in which cinema relates to the real world. In my own take here, I would like to scale down the size of the investigation and make a bottom-up start. By focusing on a single film and performing a meticulous analysis with a variety of tools and concepts, I would like to explore the details of the cinema/reality binary as it unfolds in the case of *Wag the Dog*. From the filmic texture and the story that it contains to the historical context and the conditions in which it was produced, exhibited and received worldwide, *Wag the Dog* constitutes an intriguing case in world film history that illuminates a series of operations in the way a fiction film interacts with reality. As we construe this interaction on multiple levels, we will be given the chance to assess a significant number of ideas and concepts from film theory and we will be faced with a number of questions as to how they could be reformulated vis-à-vis the contemporary cinematic experience.

Throughout the book I will maintain a dual focus: *Wag the Dog* as a specific film example and the cinema/reality interplay that is reflected in and reflects upon the film. The particular traits of the film as a storytelling vehicle and a cultural artifact will be consistently scrutinized with a wide theoretical artillery, ranging from narrative analysis to audience reception, so that the overarching theme, film and reality, becomes sifted through diverse methods and conceptual schemas. The general argument of this study is that *Wag the Dog* could be regarded as a limit case in contemporary American cinema for the ways in which it confronts us with a standard set of quandaries that emerge every time we seek to define the boundaries between cinema and reality and we strive to understand how people, either as artists or viewers, are expected to handle them. The racking focus from the micro to the macro level is meant to serve them both at equal measure; on the one hand, we will discover the particularities of the movie and its exceptional path in American culture, while at the same time we are presented with the opportunity to revisit, reconsider and, possibly, revise some of our long-standing assumptions about the cinematic medium and its relation to the real world. But before anything else, let me explain why the topic of film and reality has come centre stage again in contemporary film theory and why *Wag the Dog*, of all films, is ideal for exploring it.

Why film and reality?

Ever since the time of Aristotle and Plato, the thoughts regarding the role of art have centred on its aspired relation to physical reality. Whether art should imitate the real world or whether it should creatively add to it, is the core dilemma in the theory of all art forms. Unlike painting, poetry or music, however, cinema seemed to boast a unique bond to reality, a bond that would stir even more divisive views regarding its purported destiny. The technical capacity of the moving images to record real life so faithfully was a mixed blessing for the new medium to the extent that it immediately triggered antithetical approaches both in filmmaking practices and in theoretical writings. In what has been dubbed as 'classical film theory', a canon of texts starting from Hugo Münsterberg, Béla Balász, Rudolf Arnheim, Sergei Eisenstein in the 1910s and 1920s, and moving up to André Bazin and Siegfried Kracauer in the 1940s, 1950s and 1960s, we witness a number of oppositions and confrontations regarding the relation between cinema and reality and the necessary conditions that transform a film into a work of art. As Miriam Hansen notes, 'This tradition is often taken to be primarily concerned with questions of ontology and medium specificity: What is the "essence" or "nature" of film? What can film do that other art forms cannot? And what kind of film practice succeeds best in utilizing the possibilities of the cinematic medium?'[2]

The realist tradition in film theory has located cinema's essence in its technical ability to record real life more accurately than any other medium in cultural history. Bazin and Kracauer are regularly considered as the key advocates of cinema's realistic tendency, despite their diverse theoretical as well as contextual background.[3] In a series of essays known as the two volumes of *What is Cinema?*, Bazin explored the ontological premises of the cinematic medium, making a number of assertions that became classics in film studies, such as 'cinema is objectivity in time' and 'the image of things is likewise the image of their duration, change mummified as it were.'[4] Similarly, Kracauer's *Theory of Film* has been mostly debated with regard to his argument about cinema's redemption of physical reality.[5] Already in his *Preface*, Kracauer posits that his work 'rests upon the assumption that film is essentially an extension of photography and therefore shares with this medium a marked affinity for the visible world around us. Films come into their own when they record and reveal physical reality.'[6] A large part of his theory of film is dedicated to the minute listing of cinema's 'recording' and 'revealing functions' that equip it so uniquely in its reality rescue mission. Like Bazin, Kracauer identified several other, less realistic, tendencies in filmmaking practices but located the cinematic essence in those films that held a mirror up to nature.

In the quest of the cinematic essence, the anti-realist camp brought attention to other functions of the medium, refuting the realists' claims about the desired connection of film with reality. Traditionally, Bazin and Kracauer's views are presented in opposition to Arnheim and Eisenstein's anti-realist approach to film as art. Arnheim, for instance, believes that 'art only begins where mechanical reproduction leaves off, where the conditions of reproduction serve in some way to mould the object.'[7] In this line of thought, cinema could only become an art provided that it relieved itself from its reproductive ability and focused on its formative potential. To that end, Arnheim sought to trace the differences between human perception and mechanical reproduction, so that cinema could build on its difference from reality rather than 'its marked affinity'. Reduced depth, lack of sound and color, absence of space-time continuum and other cinematic elements could become points of departure from reality towards the formation of a truly 'cinematic' image. Similar aspirations, if more radical and politically oriented, we find in Eisenstein's writings on the cinematic form. For Eisenstein, the concept of conflict is 'the fundamental principle for the existence of every artwork and every art form.'[8] Thus said, cinema materializes its artistic mission by producing conflict through its filmic language, and particularly, through its use of montage. Throughout his numerous writings on film form, Eisenstein painstakingly described various methods of compelling each shot to collide with the next one, while advocating that montage could ultimately lead to entirely abstract correlations, or what he dubs 'a purely intellectual film'.[9] Despite acknowledging that not even he himself explored cinema's grammar to its full extent, he agreed with Lenin as to cinema being the greatest art of all, based on its formal capacity to achieve 'direct forms for ideas, systems, and concepts, without any need for transitions or paraphrases.'[10]

This lineage in film theory became the canon in introductory film courses around the world. With the advent of digital technology and the consequent changes in cinema's recording capacities, contemporary film theory was forced to review all the questions that classical theory had seemed to tackle. Despite the significant differences between classical and current film theory, such as the moderation of critical evaluations and the emphasis on more rigorous methods and systematic research, film theorists today are still compelled to address the perennial question of 'what is cinema' in an age where digital technology and media proliferation complicate exponentially the relation between cinema and reality.

One obvious strategy to begin to understand the impact of digitality on cinema was to return to the writings of the classics and seek ways to reposition their arguments vis-à-vis the technical properties of the digital. Clearly, the key problem that the digital code posed was its abstract nature and its complete severance from physical reality. For slightly less than a century, cinema had been marked by its power to embalm reality whether to its advantage or disadvantage, depending on which side of the spectrum one would be. The new material properties of the digital would irrevocably shake that power, urging film theorists to sit back and think things over. The course of revisiting the canonical texts set in motion an incredibly creative process in several possible directions, of which I would like to note three. First, and most predominantly, the effort to define digital cinema and decide whether it is a radically new phenomenon relied heavily on a close re-reading of the realist tradition, and particularly Bazin and his emphasis on film's correspondence with reality.[11] Second, looking back at the classics enabled other theorists to combine old and new theories in order to produce novel theoretical configurations. Emblematic of this strand is Thomas Elsaesser and Malte Hagener's book *Film Theory: An*

Introduction through the Senses, a title that misguidedly downplays the originality of their project, which is to explore the relation between cinema and spectator through a number of (mostly) body metaphors.[12] Finally, and rather inevitably, the trip to the past paved the way for an extensive reevaluation of the classical theories, which would take on many shapes. One of them would be to publish anew or translate into English certain collections of essays. Béla Balász' two works, *Visible Man* (1924) and *The Spirit of Film* (1930), were published for the first time in full English translation in 2010,[13] while a new compilation of Kracauer's American writings came out in a book in 2012 in an effort to contextualize the theorist's work.[14] Similarly, Dudley Andrew tried to 'open Bazin' by bringing together not less than 33 chapters, which shed light on new aspects of his life and work.[15] Apart from the tendency to contextualize the early theoretical writings, however, there were also attempts to 'correct' the initial readings of those texts either by shifting the focus to lesser known passages or by pointing to oversimplifications and overstatements. Indicative is Gertude Koch's claim that Kracauer's fame is 'nothing more than "the sum of errors" connected with his name', complaining about 'all the unproductive misunderstandings that have tended to get in the way'.[16] Without a doubt, the systematic research methods in film history and theory today, combined with the access to new materials and biographical information, will enable contemporary scholars to construct more accurate and rigorous interpretations of the first film theorists, keeping an eye to the past of the cinematic medium as well as its present and future. Because regardless of the temporal distance that separates us from them and the changes in technology and film form in the meanwhile, the questions about the relation between cinema and reality never change but are never quite the same. This paradoxical 'change mummified'[17] in the cinema/reality interaction will be the underlying concern of this study, as I delve into the story and history of *Wag the Dog*.

Why *Wag the Dog*?

Amidst the bulk of theoretical work on the relation between cinema and reality, one finds recurring references to emblematic film examples, such as *Citizen Kane* (1941) and *Paisà* (1946) as in Bazin's essays,[18] or to more recent productions such as *Toy Story* (1995) or *Amélie* (2001) as in Elsaesser, Hagener and Andrew's writings, respectively.[19] The list of films recruited for the ontological exploration of the cinematic medium is rather long and often incongruous, which partly indicates the elusive nature of the matter in question and partly demonstrates the shifting methodological toolkit applied in each case. In this book, the emphasis on a single film, *Wag the Dog*, and its thorough analysis through a series of concepts that interlock with each other, will enable me to construct a more solid and comprehensive platform for evaluating the film/reality interactions. Thus, I would like first to introduce the film in focus and then move on to elaborate on the conceptual scaffolding that could spring from its analysis.

Wag the Dog was loosely based on the novel *American Hero* written by Larry Beinhart in 1993.[20] In his book, Beinhart combined real and fictional elements in order to present the story of an American president who stages a war in order to get re-elected. The name of that president was George H. W. Bush and the war was called Operation Desert Storm, also known as the Gulf War. From within a fictional framework, Beinhart put forward his own theory that the Gulf War was merely another communication scheme devised by Lee Atwater, one of Bush's dirtiest political operatives. In reality, Atwater died a year before the war. In fiction, the problem was solved by having Atwater in his dying bed pass on a memo to James Baker, the Secretary of State, suggesting that only a war could insure Bush's re-election in 1992.[21] The film rights to Beinhart's novel were purchased by Tribeca while the script was assigned to Hilary Henkin, who claimed to have spoken to hundreds of people in Washington before drafting her political satire.[22] Barry Levinson initially turned down Henkin's screenplay but his personal interest in the role of television in American society combined with an unexpected opening in his schedule made him give it a second chance. When the filming of his big budget film *Sphere* (1998) was postponed by Warner Bros, he considered making a smaller independent production, provided that the shooting would not take long. Besides, Levinson was already well-known for alternating between expensive Hollywood productions and significantly smaller, more personal films. Once Levinson got on board, he asked David Mamet to work with him on the script, departing significantly both from Beinhart's novel and Henkin's version. *Wag the Dog* gradually became the story about a fictional President, without a name and without a face, who hires a number of secret consultants to help him handle the breaking of a sex scandal only a few days before the presidential elections. A fake war against Albania is swiftly fabricated and makes sure that the American public not only forgets about the sexual allegations but is also given the chance to admire the President's resolve during a foreign crisis. With Robert De Niro, Dustin Hoffman and Anne Heche in the leading roles, *Wag the Dog* was shot in only 29 days and with a moderate budget of $15 million provided by New Line Cinema, Tribeca, Baltimore Pictures and Punch Productions. The independent status of the production and the low economic stakes granted both Levinson and Mamet the freedom to bend the conventional guidelines in Hollywood filmmaking and take a bolder direction in the script. In fact, the script itself would become a bone of contention for all the writers involved in the various phases of the project. Even though the Writers Guild of America arbitration gave Henkin the first credit for the screenplay and Mamet the second, both Mamet and Levinson considered it unfair for the amount of work and originality they both put into the initial story.[23] The controversy surrounding the writing credits, however, would soon fade, as another heated debate dominated the public sphere about a month after *Wag the Dog*'s premiere in California on 17 December 1997.[24] The news of President Clinton trying to hide his affair with the 24-year-old Lewinsky broke in the media around 21 January and the connection with *Wag the Dog* was naturally inevitable. Yet, the 'life imitating art' concept reiterated in most news reports and film reviews alike, was not limited to the sexual element of the fictional plot. The war element soon became pertinent, too. The fact that Clinton launched attacks against foreign targets on several occasions throughout 1998 and, particularly when he seemed most vulnerable in the Lewinsky case, strengthened even further the impact of *Wag the Dog* on news reporting across the globe.[25] Thanks to these unexpected political developments, the box office of the film remained high, while its reputation kept spreading in various strands of public discourse. American politics, from then on, could not escape the shadow of the *Wag the Dog* scenario, as it became a regular entry in the US political lexicon.[26]

The textual and the contextual particularities of *Wag the Dog* render it exemplary for examining closely the theme of film and reality on various levels. More specifically, it can help us break down the cinema/reality bipolar into four separate but interrelated areas of inquiry: i) the formal level, where the discourses of fiction and non-fiction debate the role of narrative in mediating reality; ii) the modal level, where the varying material properties of cinema pose a series of questions regarding the ontological correspondence between film and reality; iii) the level of reception, where the intertextual relay of a film through mass media shapes people's perception of reality; and iv) the level of politics, where the image of the world and its potential for change is filtered through a society's approach to human agency. *Wag the Dog* is most apt for constructing in a bottom-up manner a wide conceptual spectrum, ranging from the formal to the political, which allows us to understand the complexities in the relation between cinema and reality. Given that the case of *Wag the Dog* condenses almost all the ways in which the real and the reel could play off against each other, I considered it worthwhile to subject it to a book-length analysis that seeks to provide a model for addressing the film/reality binary.

As I will argue, at the level of formal construction, *Wag the Dog*'s narration challenges the established boundaries between the fiction and non-fiction tradition, as Levinson explores the function of mediation and narrative agency, drawing on his long-lasting interest in television and experimenting with documentary techniques that play with audience expectations. In terms of the modal worries about the essence of cinema in the digital age, the central premise of the plot, i.e. a fake war against Albania, and its ostentatious shooting in a studio in front of a blue screen, are addressing the possibility of digital technology to simulate the real world and challenge our established notions of realism and reality. Moreover, the reception of the film illustrates one of the most complex interactions between a film and its surrounding reality. The eerie coincidence of the film's release with the Lewinsky scandal transformed *Wag the Dog* into a reference point that shaped the cultural and political imagination thereafter. Finally, when it comes to politics, *Wag the Dog* can enlighten us about two diverse but intertwined matters, namely the role of cultural verisimilitude in political Hollywood films and the representation of agency in political narratives. As I will demonstrate, Levinson's film challenges the traditional faith in the classical hero, opening up more systemic approaches to agency that take into account the powers of contingency and complexity in the contemporary globalized world order.

Furthermore, the significance of *Wag the Dog* in the discourse about contemporary society and culture is also testified by the interest it raised in disciplines far different from cinema studies. It became a key reference point, and often a prominent case study, in an expanded range of fields, including international relations theory, geopolitics, history, pedagogy, ethics, rhetorics, visual sociology, journalism and communication theory to mark a few.[27] Whether it lends itself as an educational tool[28] or as a model for constructivist social theory,[29] *Wag the Dog*, well over a decade after its release, has succeeded in staying opportune for a variety of reasons that constantly underpin its persistent resonance in contemporary social experience.

Overall, *Wag the Dog* is a film that became an entry in the cultural dictionary of our times because it inadvertently short-circuited the distance that is supposed to separate reality from fiction. First, it anticipated reality only too faithfully, much to everybody's surprise, and then it went on to manipulate reality in ways that seemed all too fictional. Rarely does a film probe in such undisguised fashion the dilemma of whether life imitates art or the other way around. But this unexpected correspondence between the plotlines in the film and those in the American political scene is merely one entry point into the film/reality pair. *Wag the Dog* opens up a number of other doors, which are equally fascinating and illuminating for the intimate workings of this couple in our current age. These doors will take us to discussions about the formal distinctions between fiction and non-fiction films, the conceptual and ontological stakes in the use of digital technology, the impact of mass media on public memory and the political role of cinema in a globalized and conglomerated world. Hopefully, through all these bifurcating paths, I will be able to provide new insights for a number of traditional concepts of film theory and frame a comprehensive and up-to-date study of film and reality.

Overview of chapters

In Chapter 1, I begin to draft the trajectory from the real to the reel and back by examining the ways in which narrative is considered to relate to external reality. Deploying Etienne Souriau's 'structure of the filmic universe' and Edward Branigan's 'levels of narration', I discuss the textual strategies, the institutional parameters and the audience expectations that determine the distinction between fiction and non-fiction films and their respective connection to reality. *Wag the Dog* and Barry Levinson offer the opportunity to reflect on the issue of narrative agency, while the shifting conditions of viewing of the film, before and after the Lewinsky scandal, probe us to reconsider the process of assigning reference in fiction and non-fiction filmmaking. Moreover, Levinson's stylistic and thematic concerns in *Wag the Dog* are contextualized in his 30-year-long career, as I revisit several of his films, from *Diner* (1982) to *Poliwood* (2009), to trace a number of continuities and recurring motifs.

Chapter 2 addresses the problem of the digital and the ensuing concern regarding the ontological relation of cinema and reality in the current age. Taking cue from *Wag the Dog*'s use of digital tools to film a fake war scene and analyzing the recurring situations where the status of reality is challenged, I look into the technical, ontological and semiological aspects in the debate about the passage from analogue to digital images. Furthermore, I argue that the connection of an image, either analogue or digital, to the external world is also contingent on two other parameters, namely the conventions of 'realism' and the 'regime of truth' in a given society. These two concepts embed the strictly modal concerns of the cinematic medium into a frame, which is simultaneously more specific (the aesthetic norms of realism) and significantly wider (the society's contract as to what functions as truth).

The wide lens is further maintained in Chapter 3 where I focus on *Wag the Dog*'s extratextual life. In a way, the film emulated Woody Allen's fantasy in *The Purple Rose of the Cairo* (1985) where a fictional character enters the real world and all sorts of bewilderment follow. When Clinton's affair with Lewinsky became known, *Wag the Dog* entered the news and, by extension, everyday discourse, affecting the ways that journalists would frame the political events and the ways the public would interpret them. But *Wag the Dog* had a strong foothold in reality, too. The 1991 Gulf War, the communication strategies in the White House from Ronald Reagan's administration onwards and the myth of the national hero were some of the factual elements that fed the fictional story. Once, however, the orbits of fiction and reality accidentally collided, the result was a shock realization of how these two 'entities' had been alarmingly close all along. Thus, I begin a wider comparison between a cinematic term, 'high-concept filmmaking', with what Deborah Jaramillo calls 'high concept war coverage', a practice that illustrates in yet another way the blurring boundaries of fact and fiction.

The passage from the reel to the real and back is completed in Chapter 4 where I return to *Wag the Dog* and revisit a number of concepts from Chapter 1 from a different theoretical perspective. Instead of 'realism', I discuss 'cultural verisimilitude' as a generic trait in political films that impeded the formation of a proper political genre in Hollywood filmmaking, akin to the musical or melodrama. Furthermore, I analyze *Wag the Dog*'s portrait of American politics with an emphasis on agency not as a storytelling device, but rather as a tool that helps us distinguish between diverse conceptions of action and political change in today's globalized world. Finally, I use the representation of agency as a guiding principle that could help us remap the history of films about politics. Analyzing fiction films, such as *The Candidate* (1972), *The Parallax View* (1974) and *The Ides of March* (2011), and contrasting them with the documentary account of political action presented in *The War Room* (1993), we realize once again that the line separating film and reality is more crooked than we are often willing to accept.

Finally, in the conclusion I present an overview of the multifaceted interactions of filmic and real life elements in the case of *Wag the Dog* and I discuss whether this level of interaction is something new altogether. At that point, the theories of the digital and the problem of defining 'the new' in contemporary cinema may, in turn, prove useful for reframing the entire history of the cinema/reality connection and the elements that change or persist in time.

Notes

1 Oscar Wilde, *The Decay of Lying* (London: Penguin Classics, 2010), 22.
2 Miriam Bratu Hansen, *Cinema and Experience: Siegfried Kracauer, Walter Benjamin, and Theodor W. Adorno* (Berkeley: University of California Press, 2012), 254.
3 Dudley Andrew, *Concepts in Film Theory* (New York: Oxford University Press, 1984), 19 and Nicolas Tredell, ed., *Cinemas of the Mind* (Cambridge: Icon Books, 2002).
4 André Bazin, *What is Cinema?* Vol. I. (Berkeley: University of California Press, [1967] 2005), 14–15.
5 Siegfried Kracauer, *Theory of Film: The Redemption of Physical Reality* (Princeton, NJ: Princeton University Press, 1997).
6 Kracauer, *Theory of Film*, xlix.
7 Rudolf Arnheim, *Film as Art* (Berkeley: University of California Press, 1957), 57.
8 Sergei Eisenstein, *Film Form: Essays in Film Theory*, trans. Jay Leyda (New York: Meridian Books, 1957), 46.
9 Ibid., 63.
10 Ibid.
11 These debates will be presented in Chapter 2.
12 Thomas Elsaesser and Malte Hagener, *Film Theory: An Introduction through the Senses* (London and New York: Routledge, 2010).
13 Béla Balász, *Early Film Theory: Visible Man and The Spirit of Film*, ed. Erica Carter (New York: Berghahn Books, 2010).
14 Siegfried Kracauer, *Siegfried Kracauer's American Writings: Essays on Film and Popular Culture*, ed. Johannes von Moltke and Kristy Rawson (Berkeley: University of California Press, 2012).

15 Dudley Andrew and Herve Joubert-Laurencin, *Opening Bazin: Postwar Film Theory and Its Afterlife* (New York: Oxford University Press, 2011). Apart from Bazin, Kracauer's work is also beginning to be contextualized and reinterpreted. See Hansen, *Cinema and Experience*. Moreover, Elsaesser draws attention to Kracauer's notions of 'the contingent, the indeterminate and the fortuitous' as a view on reality that resonates with contemporary experience. Thomas Elsaesser, 'The Cinema in the 21st Century. Art-Form or a Form of Life?' (lecture at Goethe-University, Frankfurt am Main, November 6, 2012).

16 Gertrude Koch, *Siegfried Kracauer: An Introduction* (Princeton, NJ: Princeton University Press, 2000), 3.

17 Philip Rosen also extends Bazin's famous phrase 'change mummified' to the terrain of 'modern historicity and the antinomies central to it.' Philip Rosen *Change Mummified: Cinema, Historicity, Theory* (Minneapolis: Minnesota University Press., 2001), 352.

18 Bazin, *What is Cinema?*

19 Elsaesser and Hagener, *Film Theory*; Dudley Andrew, *What Cinema Is!* (Malden, MA: Wiley-Blackwell, 2010).

20 Larry Beinhart, *American Hero* (New York: Pantheon Books, 1993).

21 Tom Stempel, 'The Collaborative Dog: *Wag the Dog* (1997)', *Film & History: An Interdisciplinary Journal of Film and Television Studies* 35, 1 (2005), 60.

22 Ibid.

23 Stempel insightfully chronicles the life of the script and its various versions. Ibid, 60–4.

24 After the premiere, *Wag the Dog* had a limited release on 25 December 1997 and a wide release on 9 January 1998. These dates were obtained from the International Movie Database. http://www.imdb.com/title/tt0120885/releaseinfo

25 This is the focus of Chapter 3 where I provide all the details of the political developments and the relevant media reports, where references to *Wag the Dog* appear regularly.

26 As Douglas Kellner notes, 'The phrase "wag the dog" entered the US political lexicon as a criticism of military action allegedly taken to distract attention from domestic or personal political problems.' Douglas Kellner, *Cinema Wars: Hollywood Film and Politics in the Bush-Cheney Era* (Malden, MA: Wiley-Blackwell, 2010), 129.

27 Andy Martin, Dan Franc and Daniela Zounkova, *Outdoor and Experiential Learning: An Holistic and Creative Approach to Programme Design* (New York: Gower, 2004), Stephen Atkins, ed., *The 9/11 Encyclopedia* (Westport, CT: Praeger, 1998), Andrew J. Bacevich, ed., *The Long War: a New History of U.S. National Security Policy since World War II* (New York: Columbia University Press, 2007), Matthew Baum, *Soft News Goes to War: Public Opinion and American Foreign*

Policy in the New Media Age (Princeton: Princeton University Press, 2005), Howard Good, ed., *Journalism Ethics goes to the Movies* (Lanham, MD: Rowman & Littlefield, 2008), Ashley Dawson and Malini Johar Schueller, *Exceptional State: Contemporary U.S. Culture and the New Imperialism* (Durham and London: Duke University Press, 2007), James Price Dillard and Michael Pfau, *The Persuasion Handbook: Developments in Theory and Practice* (Thousand Oaks, CA: Sage Publications, 2002), Klaus Dodds, *Geopolitics: a Very Short Introduction* (Oxford: Oxford University Press, 2007), Miron Rezun, *Europe's Nightmare: the Struggle for Kosovo* (Westport, CT: Praeger, 2001), John Carlos Rowe, ed., *A Concise Companion to American Studies* (New York: Wiley-Blackwell, 2010), Jennifer Lee Walton, *A Rhetorical Analysis of Six Hollywood films about Politics: Presenting the Candidate as a Movie Star* (New York: Edwin Mellen Press, 2008), Cynthia Weber, *International Relations Theory: A Critical Introduction* (New York: Routledge, 2001).

28 Martin, Franc and Zounkova, *Outdoor and Experiential Learning*, 154.
29 Weber, *International Relations Theory*, 59–80.

1

Wag the Dog and Narrative Analysis

The story of *Wag the Dog* is dedicated to a widely debated topic, namely the problematic state of reality in a media saturated world. The proliferation of mass media and the repercussions of technological progress on the way people perceive the real world has increasingly preoccupied public discourse over the past few decades, especially when it comes to electoral politics. Phrases such as 'shaping', 'fabricating' and 'manufacturing' reality have become the staple of everyday talk about how the media and politicians alike intervene to define social reality, according to their own interests. *Wag the Dog* puts this common knowledge to the test, and through the distorting effects of its magnifying glass, it gives us the opportunity to lean back and rethink more carefully the processes of accessing and mediating reality in the current age.

The plot of the film can be summarized as follows. Eleven days before the US presidential elections, the President is accused of sexually harassing a Firefly girl and his chances for re-election are slimmed. In order to manage the press debacle, the President's assistant, Winifred Ames (Anne Heche), brings in a secret consultant called Conrad Brean (Robert De Niro), who suggests devising an emergency foreign crisis in order to divert public attention from the sex scandal. The crisis would involve Albania, a distant and relatively unknown country, which supposedly threatens to bomb the United States and destroy the American way of life. In order to build up this fake war for the news media, Brean seeks the help of a Hollywood producer called Stanley Motss (Dustin Hoffman). Motss is fascinated by the absurdity of the assignment and swiftly begins to plan the specifics of this war, together with an experienced production team. The team works long hours to create the main plot elements of this fake news story and invent the slogans, the music theme and, above all, the visual material that will serve as evidence of the existence of this conflict. A scene with an Albanian girl refugee walking through a bombed-out territory is quickly shot in a studio in order to procure the media with the necessary visual proof. Indeed, the footage is so emotionally wrenching that for the next two days all news programmes are dominated by the horrors of the war against Albania. Oddly enough, the response from the CIA and the President's political opponent, Senator Neal, is not to deny the outbreak of the war but to announce its resolute ending. When Neal goes public to declare the end of the hostilities, Brean and Motss retaliate with the story of a soldier called Schumann (Woody Harrelson) who is, supposedly, left behind in the Albanian front. While the American public awaits the return of the war 'hero', the person chosen for this role (an ex-convict) is accidentally killed. This new setback is once again tackled most inventively by the protagonists, as they switch from staging the hero's triumphant arrival to orchestrating his dramatic funeral. Finally, the Election Day comes and the President is successfully re-elected thanks to his resolution during the Albanian crisis. Overwhelmed by the magnitude of the success, Motss wants to take credit for his creative imagination and threatens to reveal the concoction of the war. This leads Brean to the decision to safeguard the truth by ordering Motss' death; thus, their secret remains intact and the conflict with Albania can go down in history as another piece of American foreign policy.

While the story of *Wag the Dog* addresses head-on the difficulties of ascertaining whether a media event is true or not,[1] the filmic narration equally, if more subtly, problematizes the ways in which we access the story world and build credence into its narrative agents. Even though the film was clearly 'indexed'[2] as a fictional account with a very insightful tagline that read as 'a comedy about truth, justice and other effects',[3] the stylistic and narrative choices that Levinson blatantly makes invite us to revisit the blurred boundaries of the fiction/non-fiction discourse. In fact, the blurring becomes even more intense in hindsight, as we take into consideration the film's afterlife and its intriguing interactions with the political reality after its screening, which will be the focus of Chapter 3. Moreover, Levinson's approach to narrative agency in *Wag the Dog* becomes further elucidated as we contextualize this film into his four-decades-long career in the cinema, which comprises mostly feature films and a documentary about politics called *Poliwood* made in 2009.

Overall, this chapter will employ *Wag the Dog* as a case study that allows us to examine the relation between cinema and reality at a formal level, discussing the diverse modes that have assumed the task of mediating external reality on film. After presenting an overview of the key theoretical stakes in the debate about cinema, reality and filmic discourse, I will look closely at the narration of *Wag the Dog* and trace the formal elements that bring forward those stakes in the most upfront manner. Finally, I will try to account for Levinson's thematic and stylistic preferences by incorporating this particular film in his lifelong career and by identifying a specific pattern of evolution in his film language, which seems closely related to his political ideas, as those were shaped by the late 2000s.

The cosmos of film: From real to reel and back

Describing and comprehending the relation between reality and cinema is an arduous task worth pursuing on several levels of generality. For approaching the broadest level, it would be invaluable to look into the writings of Etienne Souriau and, particularly, his article 'The Structure of the Filmic Universe and the Vocabulary of Filmology', which first appeared in the *Revue Internationale de Filmologie* in 1951. As a pioneer of what he coined as 'filmology', the science of cinema, Souriau sought to determine a very specific language for studying the 'filmic universe'. With the term 'filmic universe', Souriau designated an ensemble of beings, things, events and phenomena that inhabit a spatiotemporal frame.[4] Every film, he claims, poses its own filmic universe, which is merely a variation of the more general category of the 'filmic universe' that encompasses all the types of films, despite their generic differences. According to Souriau, this overarching universe constitutes the very object of study of filmology and it should be analysed with minute precision using clear and scientifically rigorous terms. To that end, Souriau formulates the structure of the filmic universe comprising seven levels of existence that extend from the real world to the filmic world and then back to the real world again.

More precisely, Souriau's structure begins with the level of *afilmic* reality defined as the external reality, the real world, which exists outside of the filmic realm but functions as a frame of reference for the filmic universe. Then, there is the *profilmic* reality, which is the part of the real world placed in front of the cinematic camera, acquiring a physical and organic relation to the film. In the next step, the *filmographic* level, we enter the world of the film but we address it merely as a physical object, i.e. as the celluloid that bears certain technical qualities. In other words, the filmographic includes all the techniques, such as editing, colouring and superimposing that exist at the level of the film as a material object. On the other hand, the *filmophanic* (or screen) reality is the reality that unfolds on the screen during the projection time in front of an audience. The filmophanic level is at the threshold between the film as a concrete physical material and the film as representation, which is then fully developed within what Souriau describes as *diegesis*. The diegesis is the imaginary world proposed by the film and encompasses 'everything which concerns the film to the extent that it represents something'.[5] Yet, once we have fully entered the filmic world and the level of representation, Souriau considers it essential to return to the external reality through two more levels: the *spectatorial events* and the *creatorial level*. The former identifies the role of the spectator and includes the cognition, the reception as well as the effects of the film on the audience after the screening. The latter contains the intentions, fulfilled or not, of a certain creator who functions as a point of reference for the film itself.

The trajectory that Souriau delineates in these seven levels of the filmic universe may initially appear as a linear movement that progresses from an external point (reality) to an internal one (the film). A closer look into both the ontological and semiotic properties of each level, however, shows us that the dual reality/film is equally present and pertinent in all levels, albeit in different configurations. In other words, at no point can we do without either reality or film affecting one another. Even at the level of diegesis, which supposedly concerns an 'imaginary world', the role of reality both as a cause and an effect of that world should not be underestimated. In fact, the complex relation of a 'diegetic' world to an 'external' world informs a large part of a long-standing theoretical debate that concentrates on the problematic status of concepts, such as fiction and non-fiction discourse. For that matter, a closer look into the specifics of this debate is in order.

By and large, the dichotomy between fiction and non-fiction film lies principally on the purported relation between the filmic text and the afilmic reality, leading to a generic distinction between fiction films and documentaries. In plain words, we expect the former to portray imaginary events and characters, while the latter is supposed to bear a clear connection with something 'real'. Moreover, we are accustomed to some formal differences between fictional and non-fictional accounts, including different narrative strategies, addressing modes and stylistic techniques. Finally, there is a distinct institutional setting for each category of filmmaking that consists of diverse promotional methods, funding possibilities and, of course, viewing options for the audience. On each heuristic level, i.e. the epistemological, the formal and the institutional, the distinction between fiction and non-fiction has been tirelessly contested, indicating that the separation of film and reality, of art and life, is a process more easily said than done.

I would like to start my own investigation here with the formal, broadly speaking, side of the debate, as things are relatively more tangible and, therefore, simpler in that area. It has been widely acknowledged that both fiction and non-fiction films are equally *narrative* in nature.[6] Featuring a 'narrative' or more plainly 'telling a story' is a common characteristic that merely pertains to the fact that both fictional and non-fictional accounts assemble and present information to the audience according to certain causal, spatial and temporal relations. Those relations and the patterns they develop are not infinite; in fact, they have been codified to a remarkable extent by prominent theorists such as David Bordwell and Bill Nichols. The former has extensively analysed the narrative principles in the fiction film, formulating four distinct modes: the classical, the art cinema, the historical-materialist and the parametric mode of narration.[7] In a similar fashion, Nichols has identified five models of narration in the documentary tradition: the expository, the observational, the interactive, the reflexive and the performative.[8] These broad categorizations indicate that fiction and non-fiction filmmakers have historically chosen to organize and transmit their data in different configurations, equally generating different expectations and viewing schemata for the spectators. For instance, traditional documentaries of the expository kind employ powerful and knowledgeable voice-overs that seem to convey a single truth about their subject matter, while the interactive type allows the filmmaker to come forward and engage personally with the subject through interviews and discussions. Similarly, classical narratives rely on a tight character-centred causality and the continuity editing system in order to tell a story in the most self-effacing manner, while art cinema narratives grand their characters more freedom to explore their subjectivity and allow the filmmakers to leave their authorial signature on the film. These are only a few of the narrative and stylistic options that have crystallized in each tradition across time and space.[9]

At the same time, one has to be wary of the narrative barriers separating fiction from non-fiction, since formal exchanges and influences between the two 'genres' has also been noted from the start. As Noël Carroll notes, 'the distinction between nonfiction film and fiction film cannot be grounded in differences of formal technique, because, when it comes to technique, fiction and nonfiction filmmakers can and do imitate each other, just as fiction and nonfiction writers can and do.'[10] Remember how Woody Allen filmed *Zelig*

(1983) in the form of an expository documentary or how Michael Winterbottom portrayed the Manchester music scene from the late 1970s to the early 1990s in his fictional *24 Hour Party People* (2002). Particularly when it comes to the aesthetics of the observational documentaries or the cinema vérité techniques, we notice how easily they lend themselves to parody, as was the case with *This is Spinal Tap* (1984), *Man Bites Dog* (1992) or even *The Blair Witch Project* (1999). Yet, the 'blurring boundaries' argument ought not to be overstated either; common as it may be for filmmakers to mix the formal elements of these two diverse traditions, we should not understate the fact that the majority of fiction and non-fiction films adhere to fairly distinct patterns of story transmission accompanied by corresponding patterns of forming hypotheses and making inferences about the relation of the narrative with the external world.

This brings me to the epistemological level of the debate, namely how viewers comprehend a filmic text as either fiction or non-fiction. This aspect of the divide is most insightfully discussed by Edward Branigan in the volume *Narrative Comprehension and Film* (1992), which will be my guidebook throughout this chapter. For that reason, I would like to dwell on the way in which Branigan theorizes the relation between fictional and non-fictional narratives to the external world from the point of view of the spectator, emphasizing the procedures through which this relation is established. Instead of falling into the ontological pitfalls of most discussions around issues of objectivity, selectivity, bias and other modal constraints of the filmic medium,[11] Branigan starts out by making an invaluable observation, namely that both kinds of discourse ultimately tell us things about the real world. As he observes,

> A reader may interpret a text fictionally or nonfictionally, or in both ways. The analyst's task is to define what the reader is doing – what sorts of mental calculation are being made – when a portion of a text is responded to one way rather than another. *Ultimately both ways of responding (if successful) connect to the world; both are 'real' in the sense that they have the power to teach us something about the world.*[12] [Emphasis added]

It is important to stress Branigan's argument that in a final analysis both fiction and non-fiction refer to the real world, albeit in different ways. The key difference lies in the type of reference that each genre evokes in the spectator's mind. In this light, fiction is a lot more complicated than lying, and non-fiction is a lot more complicated than telling the truth. With this general premise in mind, let us follow closely Branigan's argumentation, as it sheds light on the fine nuances of the film/reality complex that will be informing not only this chapter but the entire book as well.

Starting with fiction, Branigan notes the following:

> A 'fiction' is neither simply false nor obviously true but initially is merely indeterminate and nonspecific. The challenge of fiction is to discover what it is about. Fictional reference is judged on a case-by-case basis and is ultimately decided through the filter of a perceiver's already existing (and perhaps now reorganized) structure of knowledge, or presuppositions.[13]

This passage puts forward three separate propositions about the function of fiction in the comprehension of a film. First, fiction does not represent a false world that negates our real life experience. On the contrary, it always refers to the afilmic reality and, yet, without denoting a *determinate* relation between the profilmic and the diegetic event, to use Souriau's terms. This means that a person or an object in a fiction film do not bear a direct and specific relation to the person or object that was filmed in front of the camera; instead, the relation of those elements to our real world is left to our judgement. And this brings me to the second proposition, namely that the perceiver of the fiction film is granted a remarkable freedom in the interpretation and discovery of its connections, overt or covert, to their real life experience. According to Branigan, 'an element of choice is built into the text requiring the perceiver to search and exercise discrimination in assigning a reference to the fiction and applying it to a more familiar world.'[14] Finally, this fluid and fairly unpredictable process of interpreting a text fictionally is highly dependent on the structures of knowledge or the mental schemata that the viewer *already* has at the time of viewing. This third proposition in Branigan's rationale underscores the role of presuppositions and prior knowledge in the assignment of reference to fictional elements.

Non-fiction, on the other hand, works in a different set-up. As Branigan juxtaposes fiction to non-fiction, he observes,

> By contrast, in nonfiction no initial redescription is necessary since we assume as a starting point for our interpretation that the reference is determinate, particular and unique (this is x: it exists as such). In nonfiction, our purpose is to accumulate evidence to confirm a thesis or topic whereas in fiction our purpose is to discover how the text refers to what we already know.[15]

Here, it becomes evident how fiction differs from non-fiction in terms of specificity, temporality and, of course, purpose. A non-fictional image of a person or object is believed to be the image of a specific person or object that has existed in a particular place and time. To read an image non-fictionally, in other words, means to assume that what we see is specifically determined and directly related to the profilmic reality that existed before the camera lens or, at least, to the afilmic reality in cases when direct recording is not possible and filmmakers resort to re-enactments or digital composites.[16] As a result, our interpretation of non-fiction does not rely so much on what we already know but rather on what we expect to learn about the world around us. Even though I am convinced that Branigan would not wipe out the role of schemata altogether even in a non-fictional reading, he is, in fact, right to underline a difference of temporal direction in the spectator's processing of the narrative information. When we watch a documentary, we are eager to acquire new information that not only bears a more direct and determinate relation to what is actually depicted onscreen, but that is also likely to bring upon more direct effects on our worldview from then on.

But how does the spectator decide whether to comprehend a film fictionally or non-fictionally? Is that a strictly personal choice or are there other circumstances that determine the type of reading? Branigan acknowledges a number of factors, such as structural elements, narrative cues and conventions within the textual realm, while he briefly designates the text 'as a social object'.[17] Without a doubt, the narrative characteristics of a film could guide us towards one particular direction but, as we saw in the case of *Zelig*, the shape of the narrative was not sufficient to convince us that Leonard Zelig was a real personality. Despite the omniscient voice-over and the interviews with famous personalities, such as Susan Sontag and Saul Bellow, the average viewer would hardly succumb to the truth claims of Woody Allen's film. Part of the reason surely entails the absurdity of the subject matter as well as Allen's star persona. Another key factor, however, that dictates a fictional reading in this case is the 'indexing' of this film as a 'fictional picture'. The term 'indexing' belongs to Noel Carroll and signifies the institutional labelling of a film for promotional and exhibitional practices. According to Carroll,

> Indexing a film as fiction or nonfiction tells us what the film claims to refer to, i.e. the actual world or segments of possible worlds; and indexing tells us the kind of responses and expectations it is legitimate for us to bring to the film. In short, insofar as indexing fixes the attempted reference of a given film, indexing is constitutive of whether the given film is an instance of fiction or nonfiction, which amounts to whether it should be construed as fiction or nonfiction.[18]

The labelling of the film as a fiction film or a documentary is largely dependent on the creative purposes of the filmmaker, but it also entails the consideration of the producers, the distributors and the publicists of the film. Once a choice has been made, the tag 'fiction' or 'documentary' generates analogous expectations in the audience, which are either confirmed at the time of viewing or questioned in extreme cases, such as *Roger and Me* (1989) or *The Thin Blue Line* (1988). As long as the viewers' expectations are confirmed, the stability and the reliability of those tags are secured.[19] The more, however, one begins to doubt the nature of the reference in a filmic text, the more the boundaries are blurred and other tags become necessary, as the categories of the 'docudrama' or the 'docusoap' testify.

Overall, whenever we watch a fiction film or a documentary we are constantly trying to grapple with the complex manifestations of the cinema/reality binary. Especially when it comes to historical films, the questions that seek to explore this complicated relation are multiplied. Take *Schindler's List* (1993), for instance. Its fictional status that derives from Spielberg's reputation, the official indexing of the film as 'fiction' and its wide release in hundreds of theatres, among other things, does not make it easier for the viewer to handle the narrative information. Compared to *Night and Fog* (1955), Alain Resnais' famous documentary about the death camps, the Spielberg film does not carry 'the commitment'[20] to be true to the facts nor do we expect the images to correspond precisely to the afilmic historical reality. On the other hand, Oscar Schindler and Amon Goeth, two of the key protagonists, are real persons and so are most of the locations that the story depicts. Moreover, it is highly expected of Spielberg and his team to conduct careful research into the history of the Holocaust as well as the history of the films about the Holocaust.[21] As a result, several of the fictional images portraying the life in the camps seem identical to the stock footage that Resnais used in this own account. Thus, the process of assigning reference – partially determined or determinate – to what we see on the screen is constantly challenged by both what we already know and what we expect to learn about the matters in hand. Hence, the tremendous impact in the public domain of historical fiction films like *Schindler's List*.

What about *Wag the Dog* though? Are things just as complicated with this film or is it a much simpler case of fictional filmmaking that does not demand the viewer to worry so much about the correspondence of the plot with real life? The answer to this question will come in several installments; in this chapter, I will examine the textual properties of the film and discuss the narrative cues that guide the fictional reading. Then, in Chapter 2 I will look into the 'modal' side of the debate, or the 'filmographic' level as Souriau would put it, and discuss how (or if at all) digital cinema differs from its analogue predecessor in the way the film refers to external reality. Finally, Chapter 3 will present an overview of the historical facts that preceded and followed the making and screening of *Wag the Dog* in order to reveal an exceptional paradox, namely how a fiction film changed the way we would interpret reality.

Telling the story in *Wag the Dog*

Barry Levinson's film clearly sought to tell a fictional story about a preposterous scheme to divert public attention away from a breaking sex scandal that would affect the American President's chances for re-election. It was a film generically tagged more as a 'comedy' rather than a 'political film',[22] leaving hardly any doubts about its fictional status to anyone who decided to attend its screening in the beginning of January 1998. If we isolate the filmic text from its widely debated context, which will be the focus of Chapter 3, we can broadly identify a mode of narration that adheres to some of the key principles of the classical Hollywood cinema, as David Bordwell described it.[23] The story of the film involves a very solid, classically defined, mission with a tight deadline: the two key characters, Conrad Brean and Stanley Motss, have only eleven days to make sure that the media are busy with news other than the sexual allegations of the Firefly girl. To that end, they fabricate the story of a war against Albania and guarantee that the President's 'executive action' during the war wins him the people's vote. The mission is accomplished in the finale but not without casualties of all sorts.

Apart from the inclusion of *Wag the Dog* in the tremendously spacious category of the classical narration,[24] it would be more enlightening to scrutinize the narrative process with Branigan tools presented in *Narrative Comprehension and Film*. Branigan's narrative theory is invaluable for tracing and evaluating the functions of all narrative devices, as they organize into an integral narrative. He proposes a narrative schema with eight levels of narration in order to demonstrate that the story data of a film is organized hierarchically on several levels that operate simultaneously with varying degrees of explicitness and compatibility. He writes,

> A text is composed of a hierarchical series of levels of narration, each defining an epistemological context within which to describe data. A particular text may

define any number of levels to any degree of precision along a continuum from the internal dynamics of a character to a representation of the historical conditions governing the manufacture of the artifact itself.[25]

The narrative levels that he identifies are the following:

1. *Historical author*: the biographical person and his public persona.
2. *Extra-fictional narrator*: the outer limit of the narration, the transitional level between non-fiction and fiction.
3. *Non-diegetic narrator*: a narrative source that gives information *about* the story world from outside the diegesis. For example, an intertitle or non-diegetic music that only the audience can hear.
4. *Diegetic narrator*: the information that a bystander could possess in the story world. That information is limited by the laws of the story world.
5. *Character (non-focalized narration)*: the character as an agent; we see him act, move and speak.
6. *External focalization*: the character as a focalizer; we are given the information that he/she is also aware of.
7. *Internal focalization (surface)*: we see through a character's eyes.
8. *Internal focalization (depth):* we see in the character's mind.

In the top four levels we have the presence of *narrators* (historical author, extra-fictional narrator, non-diegetic narrator and diegetic narrator), who are in charge of the transmission of data. In the bottom four, we find the characters either as *actors* (non-focalized narration and external focalization) or as *focalizers* (surface and depth internal focalization). This means that the characters also transmit information through their actions as well as through their awareness of the fictional world. The definition of narration that results from this schema is the following:

> Narration in general is the overall regulation and distribution of knowledge which determines when and how a reader acquires knowledge from a text. It is composed of three related activities associated with three nominal agents: the narrator, actor, and focalizer. These agents are convenient fictions, which serve to mark how the field of knowledge is being divided at a particular time.[26]

This passage illustrates how central the concept of 'agency' is in Branigan's rationale. In sharp contrast to Bordwell, who defines narration as an impersonal 'process' in no need of a narrator or a 'deus absconditis', as he puts it,[27] Branigan acknowledges that assigning the distribution of information to diverse types of agents helps us conceptualize both the formal and the cognitive aspects of the narrating process. Tracing the narrative agency in each particular instance in a film, or more simply, understanding 'who tells us what and in what way' in every scene is a task that the average viewer is hardly aware of and, yet, the narrative agents determine considerably the direction that our assumptions and inferences will take.

I would like to look at a number of key scenes in *Wag the Dog* in order to indicate the ways that Barry Levinson, the historical author, has chosen to present a story whose thematic core is the issue of agency itself. Already the title *Wag the Dog* hints at the problem of acting or being acted upon, suggesting the trouble one has in determining 'who is in charge' of an action.[28] The implications of the title are picked up by an extra-fictional narrator right in the opening of the film when the question 'Why does a dog wag its tail' appears in white letters in front of a black screen (Figure 1.1). The next caption contains a rather conditional answer saying 'because a dog is smarter than its tail', while a third one claims, 'If the tail were smarter, it would wag the dog.' With these three titles, the extra-fictional narrator, who stands at the threshold of the fictional realm, probes us to ponder on the subject of causation and instrumentality, paraphrasing the idiom 'tail wagging the dog', which refers to a situation where a small part is controlling the whole of something. At this point of the narrative, however, an average viewer is hardly capable of discerning the connection between the extra-fictional introduction and the fiction that is about to unfold.

What comes next is not directly illuminating either. A string of low resolution images, which seem to come from a TV commercial, flood the screen causing certain discomfort to the eye (Figure 1.2–1.3). We watch two horse riders discuss after a great race, exchanging views about 'sticking with the winner' and 'never changing horses mid-stream'. The grainy images combined with the

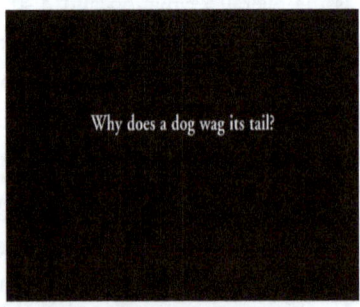

Figure 1.1

close-ups on the actors' faces heighten the effect of uneasiness and disorientation that this narrative fragment causes. Gradually, we begin to realize that we are watching a presidential spot but the narrative agency is still unclear. Is that our diegetic world? Are these the characters of the diegesis? And, if not, how is this TV spot connected to the story? In this instance, the spot works as a non-diegetic narrator that gives information about the diegesis from a higher level, which addresses only the viewer. However, the same images will reappear later in the film several times from other narrative levels. Sometimes, they come from a diegetic narrator, while other times they come as a character focalization, both external and internal. For instance, when we see Motss watch the spot and make angry comments about it, the spot is placed in the narrative from a focalized level that shows what the character is aware of and, in some cases, what he sees in particular.

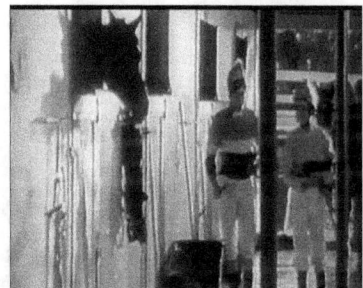

Figure 1.2

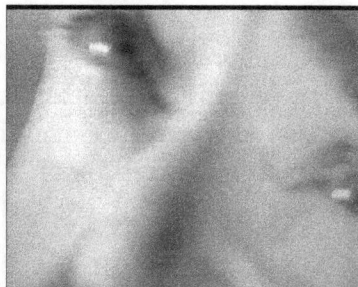

Figure 1.3

Back to the first appearance of the TV commercial, though, we realize that the narrative delays the beginning of the diegesis by giving contextual information to the viewer. The spot is followed by a long establishing shot of the White House in the evening that could be regarded as the inaugural image of a story world. The scale of that shot is immediately contrasted by a close-up shot of a vacuum cleaner sucking up the dust off a carpet, while the name DUSTIN HOFFMAN appears on the screen (Figure 1.4). In this shot, we can identify the coexistence of the diegetic narrator who shows us the vacuum cleaner in the White House and the extra-fictional information that contains the actor's name. At the same time, we could detect the presence of a historical author who chooses to create what Elsaesser would call a 'sliding signifier',[29] i.e. a visual pun with the object depicted, the actor's name and the character's mission that is about to be announced.

Figure 1.4

Similarly, the other protagonist is introduced in a shot that configures several levels of narration. As we see in Figure 1.5, the shot is divided into three composite parts; the foreground is dominated by the extradiegetic mention of Robert De Niro's name, while the middle ground shows his image through the surveillance camera of the White House. The black-and-white view of De Niro's passage through the security control could be considered as a diegetic level of narration that shows us what a bystander would observe in the scene. Oddly enough, the character narration that contains the act of raising hands and being

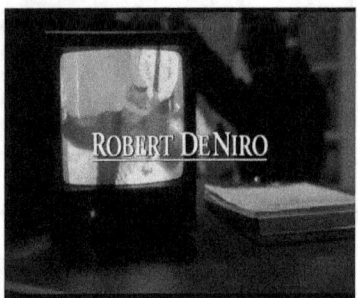

Figure 1.5

Figure 1.6

Figure 1.7

Figure 1.8

body-detected by the guard is not only pushed to the background but also appears in shallow focus, forestalling the direct presentation of the protagonist to the viewer. The enigmatic personality of this late visitor is further sustained by the shots that follow (Figures 1.6–1.8), which present him as the object of the gaze of other secondary narrative agents.

The proper introduction of Conrad Brean takes place in the basement of the White House where a secret meeting is held by the President's confidants. The shooting style of the four-minute sequence in the dark room begins to unsettle some of the viewing expectations that were established by the carefully balanced compositions of the first few moments. As the various characters sit at the table and discuss the presidential crisis, Levinson chooses to mix the standard singles and the shot/reverse shots with zooming shots and shaky camera movements, while often violating the 180-degree rule. Suddenly, one gets the feeling that the camera is recording real events, as the immediacy of the zoom and the whip pans emulate the filming techniques of cinema vérité. Even though the spectators are unlikely to read the images non-fictionally, given that the fictional context retains quite a strong hold, the narration probes questions pertaining to the sources of agency in effect. An explicit non-diegetic presence comes to the fore, offering glimpses of the diegesis from outside the story world, causing us to reflect more on the omniscient narrator who vaunts his powers. As soon as the meeting is over, the filming style of *Wag the Dog* returns to the classical path of continuity editing until the next group gathering at Stanley Motss' mansion. The brainstorming scene of the producer and his associates is once again handled with the use of abrupt camera movements and random zooming shots that are carefully weighed against the classical choices of fiction filmmaking. The selective use of these devices during group meetings works as a momentary, and yet recurrent, aberration from the overall classical style that causes us to wonder about the purposes of the historical author, i.e. Barry Levinson, and the function of the extra/non-diegetic sources in the overall narrative scheme.

To complicate matters more, Levinson himself makes a brief and extra-fictional appearance halfway through the film. The shots in Figures 1.9–1.10 appear briefly before Motss' entrance to the studio where he is about to shoot the plight of an Albanian refugee in front of a blue screen. Levinson's presence might go unheeded for a casual viewer, but the careful analysis of those shots indicates a conscious attempt of the historical author to intervene in the fiction and multiply the levels of fabrication in play in the film. Right before showing us his character in action, i.e. orchestrating and producing images that will pass off as reality, Levinson gives away his own act, directing his cameraman and crew to record the images that will pass off as fiction. In fact, the complex binary of fiction/reality, right at that moment, implodes once again, illustrating how tricky it sometimes gets to tell one from the other. As a result, it becomes difficult to determine the trajectory of the agency involved in the making of the film as well as in the progression of the diegesis. 'Who is in charge', or rather 'who is wagging what', is the question that runs through the entire narrative, both formally and thematically.

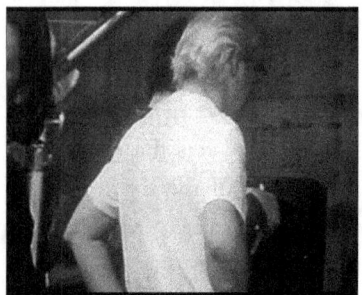

Figure 1.9

Figure 1.10

Part of the provisional answer to that question is the role of media in the narrative process and particularly television.[30] As the opening shots of *Wag the Dog* flagrantly asserted (Figures 1.2–1.3), the televised image is a narrative force of its own, working above and beyond the diegesis and establishing a level of mediated reality that runs parallel to the diegetic reality of the characters. Throughout the film, the presence of television in various places, shapes and forms, transforms the medium into a powerful player in the plot that stands equal to the other characters. Even though Branigan's schema is anthropocentric and thus privileges the role of characters as narrative agents, *Wag the Dog*'s mise-en-scène repeatedly highlights the possibility of objects to carry the weight of story transmission. For instance, in Figures 1.11 we see a TV/VCR set in the dark meeting room mentioned earlier. A White House assistant is starting a tape with a commercial that is about to scathe the President's affection for 'little girls'. Based on this piece of information, Brean realizes that his time is more pressed than expected. Similarly, in Figure 1.12 we have a shot of an airport lounge where people are watching the news bulletin about the sexual allegations against the President. Brean carefully observes the news broadcast and the audience reactions to it, scheming a way to manipulate them both. In

Figures 1.13 television again provides critical information about the plot and affects drastically the actions of the characters. Even the frame composition in this case, as in numerous others, testifies to the increasing prominence of the media in the screen space. If we look at the arrangement of the bodies and the objects in the room we can observe three stylistic details with significant dramatic effect. First, the camera is placed behind a couch, allowing the décor (lamp, vase and pillows) to stick out in the foreground and emulate a sense of the characters being sneaked up on. This staging technique is not as blatant as the zooming shots of the group gatherings but it implies a similar non-diegetic presence that observes the characters from a distance, as if trying to catch them unawares. Second, the three key protagonists violate the 'modified frontality' of the classical frame[31] and have their backs turned against the spectator. In that instance, they become passive spectators themselves waiting for television to set the agenda. And this brings us to the third point, namely that television is presented as the focus of attention through two separate levels of narration: as an external focalization (we see what the characters are aware of) and as a non-diegetic view (no bystander would stand behind the couch). The significance of the media in the story world and their power to influence

Figure 1.11

Figure 1.12

Figure 1.13

Figure 1.14

public opinion is reinforced by Levinson's stylistic choice to position television centrally in the frame. Another typical example of such framing is found in Figure 1.14, where the televised image of James Belushi is placed in the centre while the human figures are pushed to the side.

The few examples of shot composition mentioned here are entirely representative of the overall style of *Wag the Dog* where human figures and media artifacts vie for prominence. Granted, in the vast majority of these scenes the characters could still be considered as the dominant narrative agents in the sense that television or radio transmissions tend to be presented through focalization of all depths. Yet, it should not go unnoticed that Levinson chose to open and close his film from a non-diegetic level, underlining the mediated reality that lies beyond the characters' reach. In symmetry with the presidential spot that addressed the viewer before the entrance of the human agents in the story world, the film closes with a non-diegetic TV extract from a news bulletin and a non-diegetic shot of the conference room in the White House (Figures 1.15–1.16). Even though the characters have left the story world, the camera still lingers, drawing our attention to powers beyond the limits of human initiative and action.

Overall, *Wag the Dog* features a narrative that invites us to ponder upon the ways in which we access information about the story and draws our attention to a multitude of narrative sources, human and non-human, that participate equally in the shaping of the diegetic reality. The textual analysis of the film plainly illustrates how Levinson's creative choices seek to problematize the viewer about the complex relation of narrative and filmic reality, on the one hand, and the impact of mediation of them both, on the other. What Levinson could not have anticipated at the time, however, is that his narrative was meant to harbour a new set of interpretative options after a series of political developments in the American presidential scene in real life. When the Monica Lewinsky scandal

Figure 1.15

Figure 1.16

broke and Clinton was suspected of 'wagging the dog' by bombing Sudan and Afghanistan,[32] the reading of *Wag the Dog* could take, and in some cases did take, a new direction. A person watching the film in a theatre in the United States on its opening night would certainly read it fictionally, assigning indeterminate and non-specific reference to the events depicted. One was also likely to assume that these events are somehow connected to an external reality, depending on how much they knew about the Gulf War or digital technology, for instance. Yet, that connection was still indeterminate and could vary considerably within the wide limits of a fictional reading, as Branigan described it. What changed significantly after the coincidence of the film's release with the Lewinsky scandal and Clinton's publicity manoeuvres, however, is that the lines connecting fiction and reality became so much more specific that a non-fictional reading of the film was also made possible. In places like Greece or Serbia, where the film opened with a few months delay, several viewers assumed that it was a film *about* the Lewinsky scandal that unveiled the political machinations of the American presidency. Furthermore, the narrative and stylistic choices, such as the documentary techniques and the dominance of TV screens, increased the level of verisimilitude to such an extent that a non-American viewer could easily adopt a non-fictional reading of several parts in the film, despite the obvious fictional indexing and the hyperbole of the plot. In fact, *Wag the Dog* would even become a powerful propaganda tool in the hands of the Serbian people during the war in Kosovo against the American foreign policy.[33] Such was the fate of a film that modestly started out as a comedy about truth, justice and other effects.

Barry Levinson and the reality of the media

Barry Levinson made his directing début in the cinema with *Diner* at the age of 40, after spending several years working as a writer on several shows on American television. Despite his professional ties to the medium, Levinson has repeatedly expressed his ambivalence about the effects of television on everyday life. In a series of interviews published in the book *Levinson on Levinson* (1992), one can easily detect a recurrent concern about the distinction, or even rivalry, between the real world and television. In one passage, he claims that

> Writers in the past had lives. Most of the writers today have lives drawn from what they see on television, and that's the experience they write from, so it's like recycled work, second generation. Not real lived experiences, but basically television experiences. And that to me isn't interesting.[34]

Later on, he discusses the autobiographical elements in the story of *Avalon* (1990) and he explains,

> My grandfather used to tell stories. So it was the storyteller colliding with the universal storyteller, television, which would win at the end. I remember the television arriving in the house all gift-wrapped, and then years later visiting my grandfather, who was sitting alone with a television on in the background. In the final scene [in *Avalon*] there's the grandfather, who starts to talk again about when he came to America, and his grandson's child is watching a parade with balloons on television, and he's giving his attention to the screen rather than the storyteller.[35]

Given his own role as a virtual storyteller, Levinson appears to be in conflict when it comes to the impact of television on both real and reel lives. In contrast to 'movie brat' directors like Steven Spielberg and George Lucas,[36] who expressed nostalgia for the past through tributes and allusions to their favourite films or TV shows, Levinson seemed more eager to cling to 'real experiences' in his films, ignoring the oxymoron involved in this position. Similarly, he took a modest approach to film style, opting for more classical self-effacing devices and resisting the MTV aesthetics that were gaining prominence at the time. As he notes, 'the director's style is coming more and more to the fore, so that you're totally aware of what the director is doing. I prefer to discover the technique only when you watch a film over and over again.'[37] Taking cue from these assertions made in 1991 and positioning *Wag the Dog* at the centre of Levinson's four-decade-long career, I would like to look at a number of his films and try to detect a growing anxiety about the role of the media in the shaping of reality.

Levinson's preoccupation with mediation, the filmic texture and the agency of things was not central in his first feature *Diner*. In fact, this is a film praised for the exact opposite reasons; the realism of the dialogues, the emphasis on character rather than plot and the extolment of the quotidian. In a recent article in *Vanity Fair*, which appeared in March 2012, the author claims that Levinson's *Diner* caused a 'tectonic shift in popular culture' by inventing the concept of 'nothing' that would be popularized several years later in *Seinfeld*.[38] *Diner* takes us back to 1959 Baltimore and lets us catch a glimpse of the everyday lives of a group of college-age friends over the span of a week. That week is populated with a number of small incidents and casual conversations, while key events, such as the imminent wedding of one of the characters, seem trivial compared to fights over roast beef and music records. As Levinson explains, 'I wanted the piece to be without any flourish, without anything other than basically saying, "This is all it was".[39]

Yet, when you watch *Diner* over and over again, a series of other elements begin to emerge, testifying to Levinson's long-standing concern about the interaction of humans with media artifacts. In Figure 1.17 we see the shot of a gift-wrapped TV set opening a sequence in the appliance store where Shrevie (Daniel Stern) works. There we witness a conversation between Shrevie and an old-age customer about colour TV and high fidelity sound systems and we notice how older generations look at technological advances with disregard. Later on, we find another character, Fenwick (Kevin Bacon), spending time alone in front of a TV set, 'competing' with the participants of the *General Electric College Bowl* (1959) and managing to beat them all. Apart from television, the presence of the cinema is also fairly prominent, as the characters go to film theatres and discuss art movies, such as Bergman's *The Seventh Seal* (1957). There is even one secondary character called Methan who only speaks in quotes from *The Sweet Smell of Success* (1957). The fact that he memorized the entire movie and fails to utter words of his own is a harbinger of the threats of fiction over real life. The protagonists laugh with Methan and call him 'younger' and 'crazier' but in Methan's personality (or the lack thereof) Levinson expresses his fear of the effects of media products on people's behaviour.

Stylistically, Levinson tries to keep his technical choices to the background, not only because he resists the MTV aesthetics, but also because he is a novice in the filmmaking business.[40] However, a careful look discloses how he chooses to defy several of the classical staging techniques, especially in group gatherings, by keeping the camera flowing and allowing his lead characters to stay off centre or out of focus. Moreover, he avoids the classical analytical editing, which dictates the passage from an establishing shot to a closer view of the action, and he replaces it with a contrasting device: the passage from close-up shots of objects

Figure 1.17

in the décor to the characters' activity. Finally, there is a scene exceptionally staged that simultaneously betrays Levinson's virtuosity as a director and his underlying concern about how life and art may connect. In Figure 1.18 we see a complex scene set up that divides the image into two separate narrative spaces; on the one hand, we see two of the main characters, Billy and Barbara, discuss in the announcer's booth, while the foreground contains the control room where a technician is sitting and a TV set is playing. Instead of giving us a character narration that would primarily convey the content of their discussion, Levinson builds a spectacle within the spectacle, doubly framing the characters through the glass partition and by adding the TV screen on the right as a competing narrative voice. In fact, the audio track is even more intriguing, as Billy and Barbara's voices mix with those coming from the soap opera, generating a peculiar non-diegetic dialogue between the two diverse planes of fiction. In a film that strove to keep any flourish off the screen, such a scene stands out as an intriguing exception fraught with significance that would reveal itself in his subsequent works.

Figure 1.18

One of these is the aforementioned *Avalon*, which followed the box office and critical successes of *Good Morning Vietnam* (1987) and *Rain Man* (1988). In *Avalon* Levinson chronicles the life a Polish-Jewish family that came to America at the beginning of the twentieth century. With Sam Krichinski (Armin Mueller-Stahl) as a leading character, the plot presents the story of his family from 1950s onwards, while recurrent flashbacks take us back to earlier times. Those flashbacks are marked stylistically by a subtle manipulation at the 'filmographic' level, i.e. of the celluloid itself. Levinson and the film's cinematographer, Allen Daviau, chose to separate the memories of the past by shooting those images in 16 frames per second and printing them at 24 frames per second, doubling every other image.[41] The result is a slight jumping effect that distinguishes Sam Krichinski's focalized images from the diegetic reality that unfolds in the main plot.

Even though Levinson maintains the subtlety of his stylistic interventions throughout the film, we cannot argue the same about the intrusion of TV in the lives of his characters and the devastating effects he attributes to the medium. A large gift-wrapped TV set invades the living room (Figure 1.19) in the first 20 minutes and, from then on, the role of television is repeatedly noted for the manners in which it changes the habits and the rituals of the Krichinsky family. One of the key moments that underline the powerful agency of the new medium is the dinner scene in the kitchen where we watch a typical supper in the lives of the Krichinski's: Sam and his wide Eva argue about the former's habit of feeding the dog from the table, while their daughter in law, Ann Kaye, looks exasperated by the repetitiveness of their fights. Suddenly, the siren of a police car makes everyone leave their food and rush in panic towards the living room. It is not a real siren, however, that alarmed the family but the sound of their favourite show, which is about to start. Levinson meaningfully underscores the interruption of the lively discussions around the dinner table by cutting from the view of the characters sitting on the floor and watching happily and, yet, silently their favourite show (Figure 1.20) to the kitchen table that looks quiet and deserted (Figure 1.21). The gradual dominance of television in the lives of modern Americans is an element that persists through the end of the story. The

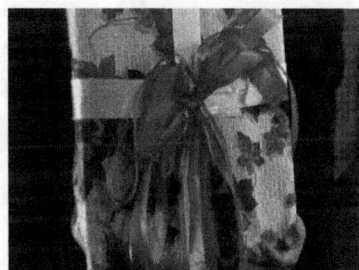

Figure 1.19

Figure 1.20

Figure 1.21

Figure 1.22

final scene in *Avalon*, as Levinson noted in the quote above, is staged in such a manner (Figure 1.22) that draws our attention to the rivalry of two diverse types of agency; the grandfather as a storyteller and television as a transmitter of lively images. Between the two, the young boy is clearly drawn to the latter.

Apart from the power of seduction portrayed in the ubiquitous presence of television, Levinson also illustrates the 'life imitating art' aspect that creeps up into all human interactions with media artefacts. The plotline that involves the children's play with the model airplane and the near accident at the department store is meant to highlight one of the most common accusations levelled at both film and television, namely the effects of media violence on young children. First, we watch little Michael and his cousins cheer the feats of the Rocket Man, as they watch *King of the Rocket Men* (1949) in a movie theatre. Later on, we see them imitate twice, once in the basement of their house and then in the new department store, one of the stunts they saw on the film. On both occasions, Levinson's framing of the action emulates the staging of the cinematic event that the children experienced earlier on in the story (Figures 1.23–1.25). This stylistic choice complements the diegetic view of the event with a strong authorial commentary, which is meant to signal the mirroring of fiction on the reality of the diegesis.

Figure 1.23

Figure 1.24

Figure 1.25

The play of fiction and reality that works as a recurring motif in Levinson's narratives becomes central once more in *Man of the Year* (2006), a film that came out almost a decade after *Wag the Dog*. The story revolves around a famous comedian called Tom Dobbs (Robin Williams), who is unexpectedly convinced to leave his political talk show and run for president of the United States. After an unusual campaign grounded on blunt humour and the satire of the established political players, Dobbs seems to win the election. Yet, his victory is not real; it is due to a technical error in the computer systems of Delacroy, the company which carried out the voting process. An employee at Delacroy, Eleanor Green (Laura Linney) discovers the computer glitch but her bosses are unwilling to acknowledge the problem for financial reasons. 'Perception of legitimacy is more important than legitimacy itself. That's the greater truth', says the CEO of the company and rebukes Eleanor for messing with democracy. After a series of adventures and struggles with the company and her conscience, Eleanor discloses the truth to Tom and he chooses to report the fraud on live television. Thus, the electoral process is repeated and the presidential chair returns to its rightful owner. *Man of the Year* ends on a happy note but not without casting a dire warning about the loss of reality in a media-saturated political world.

Stylistically, Levinson flirts with the documentary conventions even more openly than he did in *Wag the Dog*. *Man of the Year* begins with the interview of Jack Menken (Christopher Walken) who appears to recount a series of 'real' events to a journalist (Figure 1.26). Those events comprise the entire diegesis, while Menken's interview works as a non-diegetic narration that is supposed to render the story plausible and blur the boundaries between fiction and non-fiction. Even though the film's indexing and cast maintain our hypothesis schemata within the realm of fiction, the device of the testimony that contains

Figure 1.26

Figure 1.27

the diegetic events does provoke a certain sense of ambivalence as to the type of reference that we could ascribe to them. To the same end, a number of cameos from celebrities, such as Tina Fey and Amy Poehler, as well as the appearance of Barry Levinson as a TV director and James Carville[42] as a news correspondent (Figure 1.27) help further intertwine the real world with fiction.

The narrating process is largely dependent upon the use of all types of screens (computer, television, cell phones), which result in a highly fragmented and hypermediated[43] cinematic frame. For instance, the key sequence of the presidential debate, where Dobbs attacks his opponents and the entire political system in America, is communicated to the viewer from multiple screens that evoke multiple narrative agents. For almost eight minutes, the filmic images fail to focus on one particular narrative level but keep alternating between non-diegetic images and random focalizations. In Figures 1.28 and 1.29 we find a typical framing technique in *Man of the Year*, as Levinson deliberately chooses to frame the leading character in a fashion that underscores the mise-en-abyme structure of televised reality, which often becomes a reflection of a reflection ad infinitum. In Figure 1.30 we have an example of the 'reverse-shots', which feature the people behind the cameras watching the debate. Without a doubt, the mise-en-scène in these shots creates an equally fragmented impression as people squeeze among endless screens and other equipment.

Figure 1.28

Figure 1.29

Figure 1.30

Finally, Levinson does not fail to put into words his personal concerns about the impact of television on the function of truth and credibility in the real world. One of Dobbs' assistants explains at length why he has a love-hate relationship with television as follows:

> If everything seems credible then nothing seems credible. You know, TV puts everybody in those boxes, side-by-side. On one side, there's this certifiable lunatic who says the Holocaust never happened. And next to him is this noted, honoured historian who knows all about the Holocaust. And now, there they sit, side-by-side, they look like equals! Everything they say seems to be credible. And so, as it goes on, nothing seems credible any more!

Until 2008, Barry Levinson would express his views on the impact of television, and more generally mediation, through fictional stories and narrating techniques that would draw the audience's attention to the problematic relation between the real world and its image in an electronic or filmic medium. In 2009, he made *Poliwood*, a film essay, where he could finally stand in front of the camera and talk openly and repeatedly about his fears about the loss of reality at the age of electronic media. In *Poliwood* Levinson follows the Creative Coalition, a group of Hollywood celebrities, who want to get involved in politics in a non-partisan manner in order to raise a number of social issues. The documentary presents interviews with these artists during their visits to the Democratic National Convention and the Republican National Convention in 2008 in an effort to explore the concept of 'celebrity' in American politics.

Levinson opens *Poliwood* with the image we saw earlier in *Avalon* (Figure 1.19), i.e. the entrance of a large gift-wrapped TV set in the American home, explaining how this was his first recollection of television in his own family. He, then, superimposes his face on the small TV screen of that era (Figure 1.31) and addresses the audience directly with the words: 'I've always had a love-hate relationship with television.' This relationship, which we had gathered already by looking closely at his fiction films, becomes the driving force of the documentary as it delves into the triptych of television-celebrity-politics. In *Poliwood*, Levinson gets the chance to revisit several of the themes he touched upon both in *Wag the Dog* and *Man of the Year*, namely the commercialization of politics, news as spectacle, politicians as Hollywood stars and the merchandization of the political life.[44] The difference this time, however, is that he presents the real people, the real media and the real tie-in products that populate the American political arena. The similarities of the real events with the fictional are indeed striking. The result of this new crossroad between the real and the fictional is that our hypothesis schemata become immediately updated; on the one hand, we assign culturally specific reference to the images in *Poliwood* (Obama, George W. Bush, etc.), while at the same time we are invited to reconsider our interpretation of the fictional images in his previous films. This does not mean that we begin to think that either Stanley Motss or Tom Dobbs are real personalities, but that their correspondence to real personalities may be more direct than we initially expected.

Figure 1.31

To that end, Levinson's filming choices intensify the connection between the real and the fictional events. For instance, the zooming shots and the abrupt cutting that we detected in selected scenes in *Wag the Dog* now become the dominant stylistic devices to a point of distraction in *Poliwood*. Above all, however, what connects this documentary to his fiction films is the prominence of the television screens in the unfolding reality. Compare the shots in Figures 1.32–1.34 to those we discussed earlier in *Wag the Dog* or *Man of the Year* and you will notice that the only difference is that Robert De Niro and Robin Williams are replaced by Barack Obama, Sarah Palin and Bill Clinton. This type of framing of political reality in the documentary carries the exact same implications as it did in the fiction films, namely that the intervention of television, and electronic media in general, blur the lines between fact and fiction to such an extent that their distinction is no longer possible.

Figure 1.32

Figure 1.33

Figure 1.34

Conclusion

Every time we watch a film, whether in a dark theatre or on our laptop, the external reality does not cease to intervene in multifold ways. One of the first questions that we begin to sort out during the viewing process regards the commitments made on the part of the filmmaker or the production team; do they claim to present a fiction film or a documentary? These claims become initially evident in the 'indexing' of the film as fiction or non-fiction in the publicity material. The institutional tagging tends to provide, without much equivocation, a solid framework of interpretation but it is not always sufficient in itself. When the screening begins, we continue to search for cues, either thematic or stylistic, that corroborate the official indexing. Even in cases when we can easily identify the generic identity of a film and can readily secure our expectations according to the corresponding schemata, the film/reality binary still remains so complex that the average viewer can hardly be aware of the extent of entanglement of the two poles.

Wag the Dog is a film that lends itself ideally to the scrutiny of the real/reel relationship, as I will be arguing throughout this book. In this chapter, it was invaluable for addressing the complicated distinction between fiction and non-fiction at the level of the narration, which transmits data bearing direct or indirect connections to the real world. A close look at the narrative strategies employed in the film revealed how the story's thematic gist, namely 'who is wagging what', was mirrored in a number of stylistic choices that drew attention to a plurality of narrative voices. With the help of Branigan's narrative tools, we could trace several instances when a non-diegetic presence seemed to observe the characters from a distance or used zooming shots to increase the level of immediacy in the recording of the events. Moreover, we saw how Levinson made an entirely extrafictional appearance in front of the lens to illustrate as blatantly as possible how fiction and reality can step into each other's way, inadvertently or not. Above all, however, *Wag the Dog* strove to highlight the presence of television as a very powerful agent in political life in modern America, an agent capable of shaping reality in terms of its own. Throughout the film, the TV screens dominated the décor and guided the characters' decisions and actions to such a degree that sometimes it was television that 'acted' as the protagonist while the actors merely stood as props.

Finally, it was this extreme emphasis on the impact of television on the real world that drove me to examine what Souriau called the 'creatorial level' and focus on Levinson's personality as well as his other films. My inquiry into a sample of interviews and films revealed that one of Levinson's recurring preoccupations is the 'problem' of mediation, which he initially identified with the influence of television on everyday life. From *Avalon* to *Wag the Dog*, and then from *Man of the Year* to *Poliwood*, Levinson began to centre his attention on American politics, where he considered the blurring lines between fiction and reality as an alarming symptom for democracy in the United States. Those blurring lines in fiction, reality and politics will continue to be discussed in the chapters that follow.

Notes

1. This issue is also discussed from different theoretical perspectives both in Chapters 2 and 3.
2. The term 'indexing' was coined by Noël Carroll and it will be explicated further below.
3. From the poster of *Wag the Dog* (New Line Cinema, 1997).
4. Etienne Souriau, 'La structure de l'univers filmique et le vocabulaire de la filmologie', *Revue Internationale de Filmologie* 7–8 (1951): 231.

5   Ibid., 237.
6   Edward Branigan, *Narrative Comprehension and Film* (London and New York: Routledge, 1992), 192.
7   David Bordwell, *Narration in the Fiction Film* (London: Routledge, 1985). Also, note that I described a fifth mode of narration in fiction filmmaking, which I labelled 'post-classical'. Eleftheria Thanouli, *Post-Classical Cinema: An International Poetics of Film Narration* (London: Wallflower Press, 2009).
8   Bill Nichols, *Representing Reality: issues and concepts in documentary* (Bloomington: Indiana University Press, 1991) and Bill Nichols, *Blurred Boundaries: Questions of Meaning in Contemporary Culture* (Bloomington and Indianapolis: Indiana University Press, 1994).
9   Undoubtedly, the mapping of the narrative options that Bordwell and Nichols sought to do in fiction and non-fiction film respectively could be challenged for its Western-centric point of view, despite their honest attempt to be comprehensive and thorough.
10 Noël Carroll, *Theorizing the Moving Image* (New York: Cambridge University Press, 1996), 286.
11 Note how Noël Carroll has tirelessly fought against some widespread notions about non-fiction films and the problem of objectivity in publications that date back to the early 1980s. Noël Carroll, 'From Real to Reel: Entangled in Non-Fiction Film', *Philosophic Exchange*, 14, (1983) and Carroll, *Theorizing the Moving Image*.
12 Branigan, *Narrative Comprehension and Film*, 193.
13 Ibid., 196.
14 Ibid., 194.
15 Ibid., 196.
16 I will discuss the ontological concerns regarding the status of the moving image in analogue and digital technology in Chapter 2. Also, note how the relation between a filmic text and the profilmic/afilmic reality is debated from post-structuralist and instrumentalist perspectives in Carl Plantinga, 'Moving Pictures and the Rhetoric of Nonfiction Film: Two Approaches', in *Post-Theory: Reconstructing Film Studies,* ed. David Bordwell and Noël Carroll (Madison: University of Wisconsin Press, 1996).
17 Branigan, *Narrative Comprehension and Film*, 200.
18 Carroll, *Theorizing the Moving Image*, 238.
19 Steve Neale describes the institutional side of generic tags in Steve Neale, 'Questions of genre', in *Film Genre Reader II*, ed. Barry Keith Grant (Texas: University Texas Press, 1995).
20 As Carroll notes, 'the distinction between nonfiction and fiction is a distinction

between the commitments of the texts, not between the surface structures of the texts'. Carroll, *Theorizing the Moving Image*, 287.
21. Thomas Elsaesser, 'Subject Positions, Speaking Positions: From Holocaust, our Hitler, and Heimat to Shoah and Schindler's List', in *The Persistence of History: Cinema, Television and the Modern Event*, ed. Vivian Sobchack (New York: Routledge, 1996).
22. I will discuss the implications of this generic labelling in Chapter 4.
23. David Bordwell, Janet Staiger, and Kristin Thompson, *The Classical Hollywood Cinema: Film Style and Mode of Production to 1960* (New York: Routledge, 1985).
24. Bordwell initially created the classical mode of narration using American studio films from 1917 to 1960. However, he has tirelessly insisted on the persistence of the classical narration well after the 1960s and well beyond the American borders. David Bordwell, *The Way Hollywood Tells It: Story and Style in Modern Times* (Berkeley: University of California Press, 2006).
25. Branigan, *Narrative Comprehension and Film*, 87.
26. Ibid., 106.
27. Bordwell, *Narration in the Fiction Film*, 62.
28. The ideological implications of the type of agency depicted in the film will be fully addressed in Chapter 4.
29. Thomas Elsaesser, 'History Memory Identity and the Moving Image: One Train May be Hiding Another', in *Topologies of Trauma: Essays on the Limit of Knowledge and Memory*, ed. Linda Belau and Petar Ramadanovic (New York: Other Press, 2002), 74.
30. The agency of things is further discussed in Chapter 4.
31. Bordwell, Staiger, and Thompson, *The Classical Hollywood Cinema*, 52.
32. Chapter 3 chronicles in detail these political developments and the impact of *Wag the Dog* in news reporting worldwide.
33. For the use of the film the political discourse, see Chapter 3.
34. In Daniel Thompson, *Levinson on Levinson* (London: Faber & Faber, 1992), 24.
35. Ibid., 104.
36. Emanuel, Levy, *Cinema of Outsiders: The Rise of American Independent Film* (New York and London: New York University Press, 1999), 273.
37. Ibid., 67.
38. S. L. Price, 'Much Ado About Nothing', *Vanity Fair*, March 2012, http://www.vanityfair.com/hollywood/2012/03/diner-201203 [Accessed 1 May 2013]
39. Quoted in Ibid.
40. Levinson explains in detail the uses of the camera in the film and confesses his lack of experience in Thompson, *Levinson on Levinson*.
41. Ibid., 110.

42 I discuss the appearance of James Carville in the documentary *The War Room* (1993) in Chapter 4.
43 For a description of hypermediated cinematic space, see my work on post-classical narration. Thanouli, *Post-Classical Cinema*.
44 I examine these issues in *Wag the Dog* in Chapter 3.

2

Wag the Dog and the Digital

One of the key moments in *Wag the Dog* is the shooting of the war footage that signals the beginning of the Albanian crisis. Motss and his team decide to leak a news video to the media in order to visually establish the outbreak of the war. After working long hours on the pre-production of this video, the main protagonists arrive in a Hollywood studio and make sure that every minute detail of the shooting is carried out in the most efficient, as well as confidential, manner. In a six-minute-sequence Barry Levinson captures the intricate process of image fabrication and highlights the complex interactions between fiction and reality vis-à-vis the digital technology. A closer look into this scene will be most revealing.

The diegetic transition from Motss' mansion to the studio is made with a shot of a limousine driving through the streets of LA accompanied by a radio news report on the soundtrack. It is followed by an extradiegetic shot of Levinson and his crew (Figures 1.9–1.10), which I previously discussed as an example of how the film narration regularly breaks the diegesis to problematize the relation between the fictional level and the external reality. In this case, the break is all too subtle though, as it is possible for the viewer to miss the presence of the real filmmaker; the shot lasts only nine seconds and it is followed by the entrance of the fictional filmmaker, Stanley Motss, who rushes into the studio to set up the shooting. In an ostentatiously long take, the camera fluidly follows him around as he walks in front of a blue screen talking to his assistants and giving instructions to the girl who will play the refugee in the war scene. The young actress, played by Kirsten Dunst, was carefully cast for her 'Albanian' looks and appears dressed in a traditional costume, trying anxiously to understand the purpose of the shooting. Brean and Ames make sure that she will not put this project on her résumé and move on to deal with what appears to become a major issue; the selection of the pet that the girl will hold in her arms as she runs away from a bombed-out Albanian village. The production assistants have brought in several breeds of dogs, cats and kittens but Motss finds it hard to choose. Eventually, they decide to insert the animal digitally during post-production and hand the actress a bag of potato chips in order to ascertain her arm position. When she looks at it in wonder, Motss explains that they are going to 'punch a kitten in later' so that they can have a wider set of options.

The film then takes us to the control booth where we see Motss sitting next to the director in front of multiple monitors showing the girl against the bare sweep of the back wall. We hear 'action' and we see her run forward towards the camera. This simple and unremarkable movement suddenly becomes meaningful as the director pastes in the background the image of a burning village. A library of stock images and sounds offers the creative team a wide range of choices to render the video as realistic as possible. Motss asks the director to add flames, a burning bridge, screaming sounds and sirens. All of a sudden he realizes that the kitten he had envisioned for that scene is a calico kitten. The director promptly finds one among the stock images but Ames, who is on the phone with the President, objects to this choice. She insists that the President wants a white kitten and he is not willing to negotiate it. Much to his distress, Motss succumbs to his orders and asks the director to use a white kitten. A close up shot on the latter's fingers as he presses the buttons of the console is followed by a close view of the monitor showing the chips being morphed into a white kitten (Figures 2.1–2.2). Now the key ingredients of the video are all in place and the team will be able to leak it to the press over the next few hours.

The emphasis of this entire scene on the kitten that the Albanian girl will take to her rescue, starting with Motss' initial indecisiveness and culminating with the lengthy dispute in the control room, serves two narrative premises. First, it contributes to the satiric portrait of presidential power that the entire film constructs, which will be further analysed in Chapter 4. Second, it gives the

Figure 2.1

Figure 2.2

film the opportunity to address the key issue of digital technology and its repercussions on the recording of reality, which is going to be my focus here. More specifically, I would like to discuss the relation of film and reality at the filmographic level,[1] i.e. at the level that concerns the film as a material object, which, depending on its qualities, acquires varying relations with the afilmic reality. In order to understand the dual film/reality at a modal level, I would like to engage with a number of theoretical positions about the passage from analogue to digital cinema and highlight the main concerns regarding the relation of film and reality in the digital era. The overview of the main concepts and arguments in this current debate will help me analyse in more depth the aforementioned scene as well as other key moments of *Wag the Dog*. The goal is to formulate the position that this film takes on a number of controversial points, such as the status of the image in contemporary media, the correspondence of film and reality, the conventions of digital realism and, finally, the regimes of truth in a media saturated environment.

What is cinema?

> Photography and the cinema on the other hand are discoveries that satisfy, once and for all and in its very essence, our obsession with realism.
>
> Bazin, *What is Cinema?*[2]

In *What is Cinema?*, Bazin set out to explore the essence of the cinematic medium, maintaining a firm belief in its ability to reproduce physical reality in a mechanical manner. The ties of cinema with the external world were destined to become stronger, he deemed, as each new technical innovation could satisfy the cinema's inherent tendency towards greater realism. The question 'what is cinema?' that haunted Bazin is, in fact, one of the key problems that penetrate, explicitly or not, every thread of film theory since the inception of the medium. Particularly during periods of transition, the volatile nature of essentialist definitions of the cinema is more openly exposed, as technological advancements incite significant changes in the cinematic practice. Throughout film history, every major technological breakthrough would be called a 'revolution' and would alarm theorists about the new directions opening ahead for cinema. The first revolution was undoubtedly the advent of sound in the late 1920s, a development met equally with elegies as well as celebrations. It would suffice to mention the emblematic opposition between Arnheim and Eisenstein, on the one hand, and Kracauer and Bazin on the other; the former lamented the loss of expressive power in the cinematic image due to the intervention of sounds, while the latter cheered the talkies' ability to come a step closer to the experience of the real world.[3] As it turned out, both sides exaggerated the impact of sound on the morphology of the film; current and more systematic research into the formal qualities of the transitional period gradually revealed the significant continuities between silent and talking moving images.[4]

A similar historical and theoretical challenge arises with the coming of digital technology. The passage from analogue to digital cinema poses key ontological and aesthetic concerns that beg us to reconsider the answer to Bazin's persistent question: what is cinema in the digital age and, by extension, what is its relation to reality?[5] The answers vary and, as in the case of sound, they can be distinguished into those that regard digital cinema as a revolution that brings something entirely new and those that underline the persisting continuities between the different technological phases.[6] My purpose here is to investigate both sides and to trace the new conceptual stakes for the cinematic medium in the age of digitality and media convergence, when the boundaries among the different media blurred more than ever. The advantage of this contemporary transitional period is the incentive to revise and rethink some of the issues we believed to have been settled. As William Uricchio reminds us,

> But perhaps most importantly, such moments [of change] challenge the 'taken for grantedness' that under normal circumstances tends to blind us to the possibilities inherent in a particular medium and the processes by which social practice gradually privileges one vision of the medium over the others.[7]

The new technological developments at this historical juncture oblige us to study the cinematic medium objectively once again in search of new functions and applications that had been previously overlooked. My focus will be exclusively on the impact of digital technology on the films as texts and not on other aspects, such as production or distribution. The reasons for this choice are not merely of a practical nature. The digital revolution did not touch upon all facets of the medium, nor did it engage everything involved in the cinematic industry equally. The possibility for a fully digital cinema – digital production, post-production, distribution, exhibition – is still a 'question mark on the cinema horizon'.[8] Thus, the weight of the theoretical inquiry so far has fallen considerably more on the qualities of digital images and the way they renegotiate the relation of cinema to the afilmic reality.

In order to understand the ongoing discussion about digital cinema it would be useful to distinguish it into three main strands; the technological, the ontological and the semiological. At the technological level, a digital medium is easily discernible from its analogue predecessor because the key quality of digitality is the generation, the processing and the storage of data in a fully abstract code consisting of discrete electrical impulses that can take only two numerical values, 0 and 1. Thus, all the images or other optical elements that appear on a computer screen are, in fact, a numerical matrix of those two values and they bear *no natural relation* to the objects they represent. Whereas a photographic image amounts to the trace of a light beam emitted by a pre-existing object and captured by a device that is either chemically photosensitive (photography, cinema) or electronic (video), the creation of a digital image does not require the real existence of an object but the generation of a numerical matrix that will be transformed into pixels.[9]

In the case of the cinema, this technical difference between analogue and digital technology stirred apprehension among thinkers, who were confronted with aspects of the cinematic medium that had been repressed or were considered inferior. A systematic attempt to map the new territory is found in Lev Manovich's work, which defines the digital cinema with an emphasis on the continuities between the new and the old and underlines the complex interactions between novelty and repetition.[10] In his book *The Language of New Media*, Manovich's main goal is to outline the principles of the language of the new media and to identify among them the formal and aesthetic legacy of the old media. He seems to be equally interested, however, in the reverse question, i.e. how the new media in return have affected the cinematic language of today. One of the features of fiction films in analogue cinema, he claims, was the almost exclusive use of live-action footage. The vast majority of the moving images in fiction filmmaking consisted of photographic inscriptions of a real, if staged, action that was taking place in front of the camera in real time and space. Nowadays, with the advent of 3-D animation and digital compositing, live-action footage is stripped of its exclusivity. According to Manovich, the introduction of digital technology in the cinematic practice had four decisive consequences. First, it became possible to circumvent the need to film physical reality by generating film-like scenes directly on a computer with the help of 3-D animation. Thus, live-action footage is no longer the only material from which films can be constructed. Second, the digitization of live-action footage deprives it of its privileged indexical relationship to profilmic reality and cancels any distinction between the images that were produced analogically and digitally. Once an optical element is inserted into the computer, it is automatically transformed into pixels whose origins can no longer be traced. Third, the live-action footage in a digital form functions as the raw material for further compositing, animating and morphing, through which the digital film acquires a unique plasticity.[11] And finally, the digital environment collapses the distinction between editing and special effects; arranging the images in time (editing) and space (effects) becomes the same operation both technically as well as conceptually. These four propositions lead Manovich to a complete definition of digital cinema as follows: 'Digital film = live action material + painting + image processing + compositing + 2-D compositing + 3-D animation.'[12]

This definition of digital cinema and the multiple elements of the equation could be considered exceptionally innovative, if someone ignored the history of the cinema and the principles of media evolution. In contrast, Manovich deploys the new possibilities to renegotiate the dominant version of film history and to problematize us regarding the aesthetic choices that were made since the inception of the cinematic medium. More specifically, he observes that all the characteristics of digital cinema in the contemporary age are, in fact, the core elements of traditional animation, a cinematic practice that had been kept in the margins for the lack of its artistic expression. It was animation which first engulfed the manual construction of images, the graphic representation of faces and the discrete nature of space and movement, while the vast part of dominant cinema veered towards a photographic realism that sought to erase any traces of its own production process.[13] Apart from animation, Manovich notes how the same self-reflexive tendencies and the graphic spirit are also found in examples of early cinema and experimental films.[14] Therefore, the digital cinema rediscovers techniques and processes that had remained in the periphery of the medium for decades for fear of exposing the problematic relationship between the cinema and physical reality.[15] In this new light, digital cinema has brought the history of the medium full circle and has become 'a particular case of animation that uses live-action footage as one of its main elements.'[16]

Inevitably, this new approach to digital cinema as a type of animation raises some crucial ontological concerns and brings us to the second part of our investigation. As I pointed out earlier, the relation between film and reality preoccupied prominent thinkers, like Bazin, in their efforts to define the essence of the cinematic medium. For a fair amount of time, analogue moving images seemed to have resolved the issue by ensuring an indexical relation to the external world, on the one hand, and by establishing a series of realistic norms for the depiction of that world to the audience. Yet, what happened when digital technology overshadowed the importance of live-action footage or transformed it into a numerical code cut off from its original source? Can we still talk about any relation between the cinema and the real world?

Predictably enough, some answers to this question were fairly pessimistic. Remember how the famous French critic Jean Douchet lamented the impending death of the cinema:

> The shift towards virtual reality is a shift from one type of thinking to another, a shift in purpose which modifies, disturbs, perhaps even perverts man's relation to what is real. All good films, we used to say in the 1960s, when the cover of *Cahiers du cinéma* was still yellow, are documentaries, ... and filmmakers deserved to be called 'great' precisely because of their near obsessive focus on capturing reality and respecting it, respectfully embarking on the way of knowledge.[17]

Douchet's words nostalgically resonate with Bazin's admiration of cinema's obsession with realism or Roland Barthes' faith in photography's authentication of reality.[18] Along the same lines, Wheeler Winston Dixon (1995) is concerned about the loss of reality as well as the future of the professional in the audio-visual media. As he notes,

> But by far the most radical extension of digital imaging is the idea that entire films and television shows may well be created without the use of actors, sets, props, costumes, lighting, or any other physical apparatus, other than a computer.[19]

The fears and the dystopic visions for the future of the cinema[20] are clearly the initial reaction towards a new phenomenon that seems to displace not only the importance of reality, but also the human agent as the principal creator of the moving images. Ironically enough, several years after Dixon's warning, the real actors not only maintained their creative powers, but also proved to be indispensable for their digital counterparts; in Andrew Niccol's film *Simone* (2002), the digital heroine could not be technically generated without the flesh and bone of the real actress, Rachel Roberts.[21]

It is precisely this persistence of the real, but also our inexorably mediated access to it, that led a number of other theorists to consider digital representations in the same manner as the analogue ones, i.e. as semiotic constructions that succumb to certain rules and limitations. Thus, we have come to the third line of reasoning that focuses on how the cinematic images *signify* a certain relation to the external reality. Souriau's seven levels of the filmic universe, which were introduced at the opening of Chapter 1, could help us once again distinguish the modes and the planes through which cinema and reality intersect. Let us remember that a fiction film presents a diegesis containing events and characters within an autonomous story world that refers to the afilmic reality but that is not, under any circumstances, a direct recording of that reality. Even in the case of historical films, where the demand for an accurate correspondence between fiction and reality is more pressing, this correspondence is ipso facto excluded. The past is past and, for that reason, the creative reconstruction –therefore mimesis – is the only feasible solution. In more broad lines, when it comes to representation in the cinema, as it has been argued, the spectator is invited to construct 'a referent whose absence is determinant, not merely accidental or logistical.'[22] Thus, if we come to terms with the role of the analogue cinematic image as a presence of an absence, we could accept Martin Lefebvre and Marc Furstenau's proposition to cast off the anxiety about the formal or ontological identity of the image and concentrate on its semiological function. In an article called 'Digital editing and montage: the vanishing celluloid and beyond', they examine at length the significance of semiotics for understanding filmic images and scrutinize the concept of the 'index' in order to illustrate how '*indexicality is simply how signs indicate what it is they are about*' [emphasis in the original].[23] Whether it is a photographic or a *graphic* image, its connection to the real world still remains. As they note,

> Like paintings, CGI visuals are less directly connected to the pictured object than traditional photographs. Yet the computer-generated Roman coliseum of *Gladiator*, ship and waves of *Titanic*, storm of *The Perfect Storm*, or tornadoes of *Twister*, are all necessarily indexical of Reality in an unlimited number of ways, *including* in their connections to the existing coliseum, the Titanic, waves and tornadoes [emphasis in the original].[24]

In this light, the concern becomes much less about whether the object of representation existed in front of the camera (the profilmic reality) but, rather, whether this object has existed in reality (the afilmic reality) irrespective of the means of representation. If, for instance, a documentarist resorts to CGI for illustrating how the volcano of Santorini erupted 3,600 years ago, then it is most likely that those images were created on the basis of scientific proof available at the time and, in that sense, we are safe to assume that the CGI approximates or represents a past reality. But what happens when CGI is used to represent something that never happened. I believe it is time we returned to *Wag the Dog* to seek some answers.

Wag the Dog and reality

Wag the Dog plays out the distinction between fact and fiction on multiple levels and the filmic narration, closely analysed in the previous chapter, becomes a mise-en-abyme for the story's ambivalence about what is real and what is not. The significance of reality is challenged from the film's first diegetic conversations. When Conrad Brean arrives at the White House and receives the first briefing about the presidential sex scandal, his reaction is outright cynical. The following piece of dialogue is illustrative:

> BREAN: Who's got the story?
> AMES: Don't you want to know if it's true?
> BREAN: What difference does it make if it's true? ... It's a story, and, it breaks they're gonna have to run with it – How long have we got till it breaks?
> AMES: Front page. *Washington Post*. Tomorrow.

Brean is going to handle the communication crisis that will shortly break out due to a Firefly girl's sexual allegations and he claims that the truth is not relevant to him. As soon as the media publish the girl's story, it is going to affect public opinion regardless of its veracity. His role is not to prove the accusations to be false but to come up with another story that will distract public opinion until the Election Day. Thus, he asks the press officers to start rumours about the B3 bomber. When Ames says 'It won't hold, Connie, it won't prove out', he responds 'It doesn't have to prove out. We just got to distract them. We've got less than two weeks till the election.'

Brean's credo about the value of truth in politics is further revealed as he devises a strategy to construct a fake war in order to change the media agenda. The underlying philosophy of this strategy is spelled out when Brean tries to convince Motss to join the effort. Through Brean's statements, *Wag the Dog* poses a series of questions regarding the status of the image and the role of reference for the shaping of collective memory. One of his recurring arguments concerns the long-standing strategic use of emblematic images for representing an entire war, thus blocking the need for more specific and detailed historical evidence. He mentions two memorable pictures from World War II (five marines raising the flag on Iwo Jima and Winston Churchill's V for Victory) and one from the Vietnam war (a naked girl running after a Napalm attack) to prove that his plan to reduce the war to one single image is not a new concept. He also frequently refers to the Gulf War and the smart bomb footage that circulated in the news broadcasts. When Brean alleges that he shot that footage in a studio in Falls Church Virginia with a 1/10 scale model of a building and Motss asks whether that is true, the answer is 'how the fuck do we know?'

Wag the Dog's lead character expresses repeatedly a firm disbelief regarding a clear distinction between fact and fiction. The evidential quality of the image is always in dispute, as he refuses to attribute a denotative function to any historical representation whether in a photograph or a news report. Cynical as his views may be, the historical research around several emblematic images of twentieth century warfare has proven how staging and fabricating techniques have always been infiltrating the photographing process. It is worth quoting at length a commentary about the iconic image of raising the flag on Iwo Jima,

> The revered flag-raising photograph of Iwo Jima made in World War II by Joe Rosenthal alludes to, but does not record a heroic act: it is a twice-posed image made on a true site of battle that still glorifies the sentiments of many Americans when they raise their flag, and it has been replicated in a bronze national monument, a postage stamp and reams of calendar art. It incited, as well, the staging of yet another no less inspired 'historical photograph.' The Russian war photographer Yevgney Khaldai, who was Jewish, emulated 'Iwo Jima' when the Russians captured Berlin and when, like Rosenthal, he twice staged his own flag-hoisting photograph, using a flag improvised from table-cloths on May 2, 1942.[25]

Despite photography's ability to mechanically reproduce reality, it is widely acknowledged that photographs of warfare have nothing but reproduced particular conceptions of war and not the war *as it really was*.[26] In *Wag the Dog*, Brean and his team take advantage of that premise by taking it a step further, namely by producing a war that *never was*. Indeed, Levinson's characters seem to implement Jean Baudrillard's notion of simulation, so they can obstruct the real threat (the sex scandal) with a hyperreal one (the Albanian war). The film's plot illustrates how the concept of hyperreality could successfully function in the American presidential scene with dire implications for democracy and political power. In one of Baudrillard's famous passages, the workings of simulation are described as follows:

> Today abstraction is no longer that of the map, the double, the mirror, or the concept. Simulation is no longer that of a territory, a referential being or substance. It is the generation by models of a real without origin or reality: A hyperreal. The territory no longer precedes the map, nor does it survive it. It is nevertheless the map that precedes the territory – precession of simulacra – that engenders the territory.[27]

The hyperreal war waged in the film bears no relation to real events nor does it correspond to any pre-existing grounds of conflict. It is pure simulation. Even though the President's advisor convinces his team that what they are doing is nothing new, in fact, it definitely is. Surely, propaganda and media manipulation have been part and parcel of all modern warfare but the complete fabrication of a war is something new. Even Baudrillard, one of the Gulf War's most radical critics, did not argue the war was *only* simulated. In a book with the provocative title *The Gulf War did not take place*, Baudrillard claims that the Gulf War did not take place in the sense that the two opponents, the Americans and the Iraqis, were fighting two separate types of war and they were not destined to confront each other in the battlefield on an equal level.[28] This is significantly different from the story of the film, where the conflict is entirely simulated. What is even more striking is the response of the other presidential candidate, as well as the CIA, who declare the end of the conflict from within the hyperreal zone. It seemed easier to retaliate with another simulacrum rather than address the real facts and gather evidence of the lack of war activity in Albania. Again, it is Baudrillard who gives an apt description of political power at the age of hyperreality:

> Power itself has for a long time produced nothing but the signs of its resemblance. And at the same time, another figure of power comes into play: that of a collective demand for *signs* of power—a holy union that is reconstructed around its disappearance.[29] [emphasis in the original]

The signs of power, such as press conferences, presidential announcements and authoritative commercials, flood the media but the real agency is nowhere to be found. Even the people on Motss' crew oscillate between fact and fiction, between what they know as true, what they doubt as true and what they invent all the way. The practice of fabrication takes many shapes in the story, from composing a musical theme to inventing a hero and staging his funeral, but what is most emphatically portrayed is the shooting of the news footage that I described at the opening of this chapter. In that scene, Levinson reveals the process of simulation as a technological operation, which is able to produce something that never was. The enormous creative possibilities of digital technology are ostensibly demonstrated, as we watch the characters debate over which images to choose and which sounds to mix in order to make the footage both plausible and emotional. And yet, is it the digital to be held responsible for the manipulation of the truth and the simulation of a lie? Let us see how the theoretical debates over the technological, ontological and semiological features of digital media apply to this situation.

At the technological level, the distinction between analogue and digital media is fairly unequivocal; the analogue technology mechanically *inscribes* an image by registering the traces of light of a pre-existing object, while the digital *produces* an image by transforming a numerical matrix into pixels. In the aforementioned scene, we are elaborately presented with the manifold ways in which these two technologies collaborate and converge, granting the digital, however, the final touch. The actress, her movements, the cats and the burning villages are all captured in the analogue mode but as soon as they are fed into the computer, they lose their indexical relation to the profilmic reality and become a numerical code. From then on, these images can be easily composited, animated or morphed by special-effects specialists who take advantage of this 'elastic reality'[30] to create a highly deceitful video that asserts the non-factual, namely a war scene that never existed. The capacity of the digital to assert *what is not* and *negate what is* has been hailed by Friedrich Kittler, and further elaborated by Yvonne Spielmann, as one of the unique features of digitality in contrast to analogue media.[31] As the digital engages in a dialectical relationship with the analogue (the opposite is not possible), it simulates the latter's affirmative function while it performs a negative one too; whereas an analogue image works affirmatively by representing something that exists, the digital image can only simulate that something *exists*, thus performing an affirmation, while it can also simulate something that *does not exist*, thus performing a negation. The concerns that arise from the ability to simulate a negation, i.e. to affirm the presence of a non-existent object are central in the aforementioned debates about the ontological differences between the analogue and the digital.[32]

At the ontological level, the search for *inherent* qualities in these two types of images is not without obstacles.[33] The remarkable creativity of the digital tools in the making of the fake war footage appears to confirm the fears about the loss of reality in digital images. Yet, the retorts are not insignificant either. Remember how Brean questioned the veracity of some historical analogue photos, acknowledging the possibility of manipulation even in analogue media. Despite the film's extensive display of the digital means of image construction, the creative possibilities available to those working with analogue technology should not be underestimated. Granted, matte shots and superimpositions are easily detectable, but the inventive potential of staging, framing and editing a scene has been ingeniously explored from the very beginning of filmmaking, for example in Lumières' first films. In his article 'Louis Lumière – the cinema's first virtualist', Elsaesser summarizes the evidence of deliberation and planning behind Lumière's single shot, single-scene films made with a static camera to illustrate how Douchet and Bazin's belief in cinema's capturing and respecting reality had been misconstrued all along.[34] Similarly, *Nanook of the North* (1922), another emblematic documentary admired by the lovers of reality, has been painstakingly analysed to show how Flaherty's camera intertwined fantasy and myth to portray the life of Nanook.[35] In fact, a number of key documentary theorists, such as Bill Nichols and Michael Renov, have extensively argued for the problematic relation of non-fiction films to the outer world without taking into consideration any digital representations at all.[36] Thus, the advent of digital possibilities does not seem to establish a new ontological regime altogether; rather, it sets the agenda for an ontological inquiry that probes us to reconsider the history of analogue media by freeing us from the hallucination of their indexical relation to reality.[37]

In the case of *Wag the Dog*, however, the problem with the news report about the Albanian war is not located only in the digital collage but, above all, in the commitment of that footage and the break of a social contract on the part of its makers.[38] As Carl Plantinga strongly argues, the discursive function of all non-fiction representations, including TV news, is to make direct assertions about the actual world; this function is fulfilled thanks to a social contract that binds media people and viewers alike.[39] Whether a given society or a political system allows or even invites the violation of this contract is a more complex issue hardly related to the ontological anxiety caused by the digital. In Elsaesser's words,

> The question of truth arising from the photographic and post-photographic would thus not divide along the lines of the trace and the indexical at all, but rather flow from a complex set of discursive conventions, political changes and institutional claims which safeguard (or suspend) what we might call the 'trust' or 'good faith' we are prepared to invest in a given regime of representation.[40]

What *Wag the Dog* achieves is to question all regimes of representation in a political and social context that is no longer able to safeguard any of the traditional values, like truth or trust, but rather establishes a permanent sense of instability where fact and fiction are woven into a web of infinite regression. Ironically enough, as I will show in Chapter 3, the film's central premise would soon be corroborated by real life when the political developments and the fictional plot got caught in a double bind to such an extent that one could no longer ascertain who was wagging whose tail.

Realism and the regimes of truth

The social contract that dictates an invested belief in the correspondence between an image and a real-life referent either in fiction or non-fiction is contingent upon another type of contract that defines the manner in which this correspondence will come about. The name of that second contract is 'realism' and it amounts to a set of conventions that determine how and why an image appears to be truthful and authentic. If we leave the technological distinctions between analogue and digital media aside, and if we suspend our fears for the loss of reality in the digital age, we must begin to inquire into the new, or possibly old, ways that the digital tools provide for portraying the real world. Here, things once again become complicated.

First and foremost, let us adopt as an axiom what Elsaesser has claimed about realism, namely that it is 'infinitely corruptible through repetition'.[41] In addition, Dudley Andrew's following observation helps us set the ground for our discussion: 'Whereas "realism" appears to be a zero degree of cinematic representation (one involving no marked labor), we have seen how dependent it is on conventions and habit.'[42] What Andrew calls 'a zero degree of representation' refers to the classical realism of Hollywood films, which Bazin had praised so fervently for the transparency and the credibility of the depth of field and the continuity editing, among other things. The approach of the cinematic frame as 'a window to the outer world' led an entire cinematic practice, the classical Hollywood cinema, to adopt a series of technical and stylistic choices that could ensure an illusory perspective and hide all traces of construction. Indeed, the success and the promulgation of that approach were such that they could not be undercut even by the powers of digital technology. Thus, oddly enough, the new tools not only respected the foundations of classical realism, but also reinforced them significantly by uniting their strengths to achieve an even more persuasive immediacy. Hence the verisimilitude of the waves in *Titanic* and the tornados in *Twister*, to remember some of the previous examples. According to Warren Buckland, 90 per cent of the special effects used in the film industry are 'invisible' effects that simulate real conditions and try to pass unnoticed by the spectators.[43] One such famous and widely discussed example is found in the opening sequence of *Forrest Gump* (1994), where we watch a feather floating in the wind. The feather appears entirely real since it blends perfectly into the setting, and there is nothing in the spatiotemporal coordinates of the frame to suggest that the feather was not part of the profilmic reality. The special effects team at Industrial Light and Magic who worked on this film have described the way the digital tools helped them visualize the flight of this feather, which could not have taken place in reality. They shot a real feather against a blue background in multiple positions and then they employed the techniques of morphing and compositing to create an image that never existed in live action.[44] This example is indicative of the widespread tendency to put digital techniques at the service of the classical realist conventions that rely on a seamless representation of the story. What is impressive, indeed, in this digital obsession with the illusion of verisimilitude is the fact that it simulates even the slightest trait of analogue recording, such as the motion blur. In live action the movement of people and objects is always slightly blurred, which becomes more evident in moments of fast movement. On the other hand, when this movement is produced on a computer via stop-motion animation, the blur is not possible; no matter how fast an object moves, its image is always pin sharp since it stems not from a natural recording but from a numerical code. To handle this discrepancy between analogue and digital movement, the software of digital processing provides the addition of this motion blur as an invisible special effect that reinforces the illusion of live action.[45] The 'motion blur effect' is an emblematic case of 'remediation', a term introduced by Jay David Bolter and Richard Grusin to describe the perennial tendency of the media to represent other media. Here, the digital medium remediates the analogue by reproducing the motion blur, which constitutes an inherent characteristic of analogue recording.[46] The purpose of the remediation here is to establish the aesthetics of immediacy and to erase any trace of mediation of reality.[47]

So far we have established that digital technology conforms all too obediently to the tenets of classical realism that Bazin considered to embalm reality. The zero degree of representation or, put differently, the logic of immediacy is the one that prevails in mainstream representational practices, including the news video reports. In this light, *Wag the Dog* portrays most accurately the conventions and habits that news reporters employ in their labour in order to offer viewers a credible and coherent view of this world. Without a doubt, the satiric impulse and the hyperbole of the comic motivation puts a magnifying glass on the processes of image construction, but the notion of realism that the image makers convey is fairly accurate. Motss and his team constructed the video based on the conventions of what Steve Neale calls 'generic' and 'cultural verisimilitude'[48] in order to make sure that the public does not doubt the veracity of the war report. The cultural verisimilitude entails all the team decisions regarding what comes across as 'Albanian', such as the traditional costume and the looks of the actress. On the other hand, the generic verisimilitude involves both the form of the news report (brief scenes on location) and the classical story format (causality, spatiotemporal continuity) that the audience have grown familiar with from Hollywood films.[49] The story space (village, rubble, burning bridge, etc.) and the character (Albanian girl) are blended in a seamless environment that leaves no trace of its fictional provenance. The digital tools fully obey the logic of immediacy, making sure that the digital insertions (kitten, village, flames) respect the spatiotemporal unity as well as the principles of the classical realist frame, i.e. character centrality, modified frontality and depth of field.[50]

Wag the Dog shows us the contemporary preference for immediacy in several other ways that extend well beyond the staged war report. The logic of immediacy is equally propagated through the notion of surveillance that becomes significant in the filmic narration from the film's opening moments. The introduction of Conrad Brean, as I argued in the previous chapter, is made through an intricate shot that shows him pass through the security check at the White House (Figure 1.5). The foregrounding of the surveillance image and the simultaneous appearance of the character in the same frame point to the 'real time' aspect of the surveillance transmission and boost the reality effect of the situation. The use of surveillance images continues throughout Brean's walk towards the private conference room and it is symmetrically repeated during his exit from the White House after the meeting is over. Apart from this blatant use of surveillance at the opening of the film, the narration frequently emulates the sense of surveillance over the action through the multiple high angle shots in Motss' Hollywood mansion (Figure 2.3). Levinson's stylistic peculiarity is intriguing for the way it brings out the problem of realism and indexicality. The display of the surveillance aesthetics in *Wag the Dog* strives to complicate in yet another way the relation between the real and its representation. In his article 'Rhetoric of the temporal index: surveillance narration and the cinema of "real time"', Thomas Levin explores the manner in which contemporary films have incorporated the rhetoric of surveillance both at a formal and thematic level in order to compensate for the endangerment of reality in the digital age. It is worth quoting at length his main argument:

> When one sees what one takes to be a surveillance image, one does not usually ask if it is 'real' (this is simply assumed) but instead attempts to establish whether 'the real' that is being captured by the camera is being recorded or is simply a closed-circuit 'real time' feed. This is precisely what gives these sorts of images their semiotic appeal. If the unproblematic referentiality of cinematic photograms is under siege, it makes great sense to start appropriating a type of imaging characterized by definition (at least according to a certain popular understanding) in terms of its seemingly unproblematic, reliable referentiality. Surveillance images are always images *of* something (even if that something is very boring) and thus the turn to surveillance in recent cinema can be understood as a form of *semiotic compensation*.[51] [emphasis in the original]

Wag the Dog's multifaceted interplay between fact and fiction puts the concept of surveillance in the game to underline the significance of 'real time' images in the attribution of authenticity. Surveillance images imply both the sense of a real presence as well as the temporal immediacy of the transmission, satisfying some of our contemporary expectations regarding realism.

The film's major investment in realism, however, depends on the ubiquitous presence of television. In *Wag the Dog*, the television images enter the diegesis in numerous different ways depending on their relation to the story events. First, there are moments, such as the very first shot of the film, when the TV

Figure 2.3

screen takes over the entire frame, creating a feeling of uneasiness due to the low resolution of the image (Figures 1.2–1.3). Second, there are scenes where the TV set is part of the setting and interacts with the characters. Third, there is the use of news bulletins or TV shows in the soundtrack providing information about the story development. Finally, there are cases when the TV set appears in the background performing a 'phatic' function.[52]

Let's look at some key scenes where the role of television is instrumental for the progress of the plot and cultivates the sense of immediacy that comes with the 24-hour live news coverage. When Brean and Ames wait at O' Hare Airport for their flight to Los Angeles on their way to meet the Hollywood producer, the television screen in the airport lounge broadcasts the breaking news of the Firefly girl's sexual allegations against the President. Brean registers the people's reactions and realizes how time is pressing them to change the subject on the news. Ames, on the other hand, is already giving instructions on her cell phone to the people at the President's press office to deny the rumours about the B3 bomber. Levinson crosscuts between the trajectory of the two protagonists and the trajectory of the breaking story in the media; by the time Brean and Ames arrive at the Hollywood mansion, the film has shown us excerpts from the statement of the President's political opponent, Senator Neal, and a clip from a news programme commenting on the possible effect of the scandal on election polls. Television's immediate transmission of information and access to the public is what sets the tempo for the characters and puts enormous pressure on their scheme.

The strategic importance of immediacy in contemporary media reality is emphatically portrayed in the scene where Brean and Ames demonstrate their powers over the White House spokesman, John Levy (Figure 1.13). In their effort to convince Motss to help them divert public attention from the scandal, they flaunt the immediacy and speed with which they can affect political procedures. When all three main characters start watching the press conference, which is broadcast live from the White House, Motss asks 'How close are you to this thing?' Brean immediately takes out his cell phone and starts dialling up a number, asking Motss 'What do you want the kid to say?' Motss replies 'Have him say, "I know we're all concerned for the President, I'm sure that our hopes and prayers are with him"'. Ames takes the cell phone from Brean and gives the exact instruction. A second later we see Levy on the TV screen holding his hand to his earphone and then we hear him utter rather self-consciously 'I just want to say I know we're all concerned for the President ... our hopes and prayers are with him.' Motss is impressed by 'how close' Brean and Ames are to the event, but expresses his disappointment about the way Levy delivered his lines.

This scene is particularly revealing on several counts because it bears significant political and technological implications. The political dimension will be elaborated on in subsequent chapters, so here I would like to dwell on the technological side and its impact on our notions of realism and authenticity. One of the defining aspects of television is liveness. As Mary Ann Doane observes, 'While the realism of film is defined largely in terms of space, that of television is conceptualized in terms of time (owing to its characteristic of "liveness", presence and immediacy).'[53] The inherent capacity of television to broadcast live carries a promise of authenticity and truthfulness. The audience is most likely to regard something as true if it is broadcast on TV, despite the reservations and the warnings that have been repeatedly voiced by scientists or scholars. In fact, the latter have underlined two compelling paradoxes regarding the relation between television and reality. First, news programmes, the quintessence of live television, comprise news reports that rely heavily on editing in order to present a coherent account of the story. In rare cases, when news images are broadcast directly as they are shot, they hardly make any sense.[54] The same applies to the news commentary which always presupposes a minimum drafting before the journalist addresses the audience. In other words, there is never 100 per cent live television and, on those rare occasions that 100 per cent liveness occurs, the result is always disconcerting. Hence Motss' reaction of disapproval of Levy's performance that I described above. The second paradox regarding the live aspect of television brings us back to the discussion about the digital that has occupied us throughout this chapter. On the one hand, we are aware of the technical means of image manipulation and how they have infiltrated all television genres. On the other, we still cling to the idea of immediacy and referentiality, which is evident not only in our persistent faith in news programming but also in the thriving of reality TV shows.[55]

Thus, we have come to the final concept that we will address in this chapter, namely the regime of truth in contemporary Western society. The 'regime of truth' is a concept found in the writings of Michel Foucault and it could help us conclude several of the issues that we have discussed so far. It is worth quoting at some length the way Foucault conceptualizes the regime of truth. As he writes,

> Each society has its regime of truth, its 'general politics' of truth: that is, the types of discourse which it accepts and makes function as true; the mechanisms

and instances which enable one to distinguish true and false statements, the means by which each is sanctioned; the techniques and procedures accorded value in the acquisition of truth; the status of those who are charged with saying what counts as true.[56]

Wag the Dog's entire narrative is dedicated to the depiction of the regime of truth in American contemporary society. Its comic tagline[57] already hints at the truth merely being another 'special effect'. This effect is produced by the media, and particularly television, through the paradoxical combination of two elements; the enormous creativity in image construction and the ubiquity of live broadcasting. The contradictions that stem from this paradox become palpable every time the film discloses the 'techniques and procedures accorded value in the acquisition of truth' in contemporary America. For instance, the schizophrenic ambivalence captured in the conversation between Brean, Ames and the CIA agent, Mr Young, is indicative of the conflict between old regimes and new regimes of truth. Let us look at the dialogue.

> MR YOUNG: Two things I know to be true. There is no difference between good flan and flan. And there is no war. Guess who I am.
> AMES: I would like to point out that I am under medical care ... and taking medication ... side effects ... (mumbles)
> MR YOUNG: Quite touching.
> AMES: And I take this opportunity to suggest that, equally, I admit to nothing, and that I would like my lawyer present.
> MR YOUNG: We show, and N.S.A. confirms, there are no nuclear devices on the Canadian border. There are no nuclear devices in Albania. Albania has no nuclear capacity. Our spy satellites show no secret terrorist training camps in the Albanian Hinterland. The Border Patrol, the F.B.I., the R.C.M.P. report no repeat no untoward activity along our picturesque Canadian Border. The Albanian Government is screaming its defence, the world is listening. There is no War.
> BREAN: Of course there's a war. I'm watching it on Television.

In this scene we hear the CIA agent appeal to the traditional mechanisms that enable one to distinguish between something true and something false; he argues that the satellites, the FBI and, of course, the Albanian officials deny the existence of any war situation and, therefore, there can be no war. On the other hand, Brean challenges these verification procedures by evoking the power of television to ascertain the ontology of the conflict. As their conversation continues into a more philosophical terrain, touching upon issues such as 'why people go to war', Brean seems to make his point more and more clear. At the end of this meeting, Mr Young and the film's protagonists shake hands and share smiles, having reached a tacit agreement about the ongoing war: the war is on as long as it is on TV.

Then, it comes as no surprise to the audience that the CIA chooses to end the war with the only means available to them, i.e. a TV statement from the President's opponent, who looks at the camera and says: 'I've just gotten word that the situation in Albania is resolved. That it is resolved. The CIA confirms that our troops, along the Canadian Border, and overseas are standing down ...' Once this statement is aired, Brean and his team cannot but solemnly accept the end of the war in Albania and start preparing the aftermath of the war that involves the rescue of a soldier left behind.

The celebration of TV's liveness as a marker for what is real and what is not, combined with the power of the classical realist conventions that I discussed earlier, lead us to conclude that the regime of truth in American society clings strongly to the notion of immediacy as the type of discourse that comes closest to the real. Despite the sophistication of new media techniques and our growing awareness of the processes of mediation and image manipulation, the impact of immediacy is still remarkably immense. Jay David Bolter considers the persistent desire for transparency as a sign of conservatism in American society, which finds it more reassuring to invest its belief in a transparent and unified representation of the world rather than a fragmented and hybrid one.[58] On the other hand, Gerard Gaylard adopts a broader scope, noting that 'cultures are perpetually in oscillation, or at least subject to wave-like ebbs and flows, with the rush to new and potentially less representational forms invariably precipitating a resurgence of normative realisms.'[59]

Overall, behind *Wag the Dog*'s outrageous narrative premise (a fake war against Albania as a diversion from a presidential sex scandal) and in spite of the generic elements of the comedy (hyperbole and wit), the film crafts a very sophisticated account of the paradoxes and the contradictions in the way American society is negotiating its regime of truth and the stakes of that negotiation for the function of another regime, namely democracy.

Conclusion

In this chapter, I tried to analyse *Wag the Dog* in relation to one of the central issues on the agenda of contemporary film theory, which is the impact of digital technology on the ontology of film. Taking cue from one of the film's most prominent scenes, the construction of a fake news report about a non-existent war, I explored a number of key positions regarding the relation of film and reality in the digital era. By distinguishing the theoretical arguments into three intertwining areas (the technological, the ontological and the semiological), I was able to sort out a number of misunderstandings and overstatements regarding the new phase that the cinema has entered.

At the technological level, the distinction between analogue and digital images is considerably easier to handle thanks to the clear differences in the way in which the two technical means produce, store and display images. What is significant, however, is the way the two technologies collaborate; on the one hand, the digital relies on the analogue for its informational wealth, while on the other, it disconnects it from its roots in reality. Once an analogue image enters the digital platform, it becomes a code just like any other. The fact that this code is cut off from any indexical relation to a real object was initially regarded as alarming. The loss of the real world in front of the cinematic camera seemed to shatter the Bazinian vision of total cinema. Indeed, the inquiry into the ontology of the digital, which still remains a largely unresolved issue among thinkers, unsettled several of our assumptions about the connection between a filmic image and the afilmic reality. With the help of semiology, this growing insecurity was in some way contained. If we approach a digital image as a representation, i.e. a semiotic construction, a part of our anxiety is relieved or perhaps displaced; instead of worrying about whether the referent of the image actually existed during the process of recording (at the profilmic level), we should begin to question the commitment of the image and the institutional warrants available for the existence of that referent. And it is precisely to that point that *Wag the Dog* led us with its highly intricate play of images, its multiple modalities and its persistent questions about the meaning of reality.

Wag the Dog's creators managed to incorporate in the film's story and narration all the central concerns that arose from the advent of digital media and they were remarkably successful at striking the contradictions of contemporary visual culture. One of Motss' final lines is 'It's a complete fucking fraud and it looks 100 per cent real. It's the best work I've ever done in my life because it's so honest.' His pride as well as his emotional engagement with the war project shows how corrosive the power of fiction can be for someone who has spent his life in a dream factory. The film, on the other hand, stands undivided. The closure takes a crystal clear stance in the fact/fiction complex, *at least* with respect to reality's ontological status; truth does exist and Motss has to die to protect it. After spending an hour and a half exposing the workings of hyper-reality and media manipulation, *Wag the Dog* reminds us of two traditional values, such as reality and human agency. The scene where Brean orders Motss' sacrifice with a simple wave of his hand is illustrative of two aspects; first, reality is always potentially verified and, therefore, never lost altogether. Second, the responsibility for an action, in this case the murder, is located in a specific individual who has the power over somebody else's life. Even though the power of fiction and the disembodied power of politics dominated the diegesis from the opening moments of the film, *Wag the Dog* dropped the curtain with the reinstatement of two key modernist notions, namely objectivity and subjectivity.[60] This meant that Levinson and his writers, despite their wild imagination, did not see 'reality' coming.

Notes

1 I maintain Souriau's 7 levels of the filmic universe, presented in Chapter 1, as a guideline for addressing the relation between cinema and reality throughout this book.
2 André Bazin, *What is Cinema?* Vol. I (Berkeley: University of California Press, [1967] 2005), 12.
3 The broader opposition between these theorists on the desired relation between cinema and reality is briefly discussed in the Introduction. Rudolf Arnheim, *Film as Art* (Berkeley: University of California Press, 1957); Sergei Eisenstein, *Film Form: Essays in Film Theory*, trans. Jay Leyda (New York: Meridian Books, 1957); Siegfried Kracauer, *Theory of Film: The Redemption of Physical Reality* (Princeton, NJ: Princeton University Press, 1997); André Bazin, *What is Cinema?*.
4 Close narrative studies have shown that the coming of sound did not affect the narrative construction of films as much as it is commonly regarded. Instead, a major break in the storytelling techniques had taken place earlier, in the period 1906–17, when we moved from 'early cinema' to the 'cinema of narrative integration'. David Bordwell, Janet Staiger, and Kristin Thompson, *The Classical Hollywood Cinema: Film Style and Mode of Production to 1960* (New York:

Routledge, 1985); Thomas Elsaesser, *Early Cinema: Space Frame Narrative* (London: BFI, 1990).

5   My focus is mainly on the cinema, but the same issues apply to all analogue visual media, such as photography and television.

6   An answer is found in Dudley Andrew's latest volume entitled *What Cinema Is!* Apart from his own position on what cinema is, Andrew also provides a new reading of Bazin's work. Dudley Andrew, *What Cinema Is!* (Malden, MA: Wiley-Blackwell, 2010).

7   William Uricchio, 'Historicizing media in transition', in *Rethinking Media Change: The Aesthetics of Transition*, ed. David Thorburn and Henry Jenkins (Cambridge, Massachusetts: MIT Press, 2003), 31.

8   John Belton, 'Digital Cinema: A False Revolution', *October* 100 (2002): 110.

9   Lucia Santaella-Braga, 'The prephotographic, the photographic, and the postphotographic image', in *Semiotics of the Media. State of the Art, Projects, and Perspectives*, ed. Winfried Nöth (Berlin and New York: Mouton de Gruyter, 1997), 121.

10 Lev Manovich, *The Language of New Media* (Cambridge, MA: MIT Press, 2001).

11 In addition to Manovich's observation, we can also consider William Mitchell's argument regarding the plasticity of digital images. As he notes, 'the essential characteristic of digital information is that it can be manipulated easily and very rapidly by a computer. It is simply a matter of substituting new digits for old. Digital images are, in fact, much more susceptible to alteration than photographs, drawings, paintings, or any other kinds of images.' [emphasis in the original]. William J. Mitchell, *The Reconfigured Eye. Visual Truth in the Post-Photographic Era* (Cambridge, MA: MIT Press, 1992), 7.

12 Manovich, *The Language of New Media*, 301.

13 Ibid., 298.

14 This fact confirms Jenkins and Thorburn's view that 'in some instances the earliest phase of a medium's life may be its most artistically rich, as pioneering artists enjoy a freedom to experiment that may be constrained by the conventions and routines imposed when production methods are established.' Henry Jenkins and David Thorburn, 'Introduction: Toward an Aesthetics of Transition', in *Rethinking Media Change: The Aesthetics of Transition*, ed. Henry Jenkins and David Thorburn (Cambridge, MA: MIT Press, 2003), 6.

15 The practices of experimental cinema, which principally aim at challenging the conventions of realism and narrative, were named 'proto-digital' by Malcolm Le Grice. Malcolm LeGrice, *Experimental Cinema in the Digital Age* (London: BFI, 2001), 316.

16 Manovich, *The Language of New Media*, 302.

17 Douchet in Thomas Elsaesser, 'Early Film History and Multi-media: An Archaeology of Possible Futures?' in *New Media, Old Media: A History and Theory Reader*, ed. Wendy Hui Kyong Chun and Thomas Keenan (New York: Routledge, 2005), 14.
18 For a comparison between Bazin and Barthes' views, see Colin MacCabe, 'Barthes and Bazin: The Ontology of the Image', in *Writing the Image after Roland Barthes*, ed. Jean-Michel Rabaté (Philadelphia: University of Pennsylvania Press, 1997).
19 Wheeler Winston Dixon, 'The Digital Domain: Image Mesh and Manipulation in Hyperreal Cinema/Video', *Film Criticism* 20, 1/2 (1995): 63.
20 We find the same concerns across the entire spectrum of audiovisual culture and the writings of Baudrillard, Virilio and Vattimo are fairly indicative. For an overview of their arguments, see Sean Cubitt, 'Phalke, Méliès, and special effects today', *Wide Angle* 21, 1 (1999).
21 The alternative title of this film is *S1m0ne* to indicate the numerical code of digital technology that transforms all signals into combinations of the digits 1 and 0.
22 Dudley Andrew, *Concepts in Film Theory* (New York: Oxford University Press, 1984), 45.
23 Martin Lefebvre and Marc Furstenau, 'Digital editing and montage: the vanishing celluloid and beyond', *CiNéMAS* 13, 1-2 (2002): 97.
24 Lefebvre and Furstenau, 'Digital editing and montage', 99.
25 Eugene Vance, 'The Past as Text and the Historiography of Tomorrow: Notes on a Recent Book', *MLN* 113, 4 (1998): 958. Error in date in original. The correct date is May 2, 1945.
26 Bernd Hüppauf, 'Experiences of Modern Warfare and the Crisis of Representation', *New German Critique* 59 (1993).
27 Jean Baudrillard, *Simulacra and simulation* (Ann Arbor: The University of Michigan Press, 1994), 1.
28 Jean Baudrillard, *The Gulf War Did Not Take Place* (Bloomington: Indiana University Press, 1995).
29 Jean Baudrillard, *Simulacra and simulation*, 23.
30 Lev Manovich notes that the privilege of this type of elastic reality, i.e. analogue images in a digital platform, is that 'while retaining the visual realism unique to the photographic process, film obtains a plasticity that was previously only possible in painting or animation'. Manovich, *The Language of New Media*, 301.
31 Friedrich Kittler, 'Fiktion und Simulation', in *Philosophien der neuen Technologie*, ed. Ars Electronica (Berlin: Merve Publishers, 1989) and Yvonne Spielmann, 'Aesthetic features in digital imaging: collage and morph', *Wide Angle* 21, 1 (1999).
32 Kittler and Spielmann identify a third type of image, the electronic, that stands

between the analogue and the digital. Whereas the electronic is analogue in principle, it prefigures several qualities of the digital. Spielmann, 'Aesthetic features in digital imaging' and Friedrich Kittler, *Optical Media* (Cambridge: Polity Press, 2010).

33 Despite the differences among visual forms so diverse as photographs, fiction films, documentaries and TV news, the theoretical inquiry into the impact of digital technology on their formal and ideological functions seems to follow – paradoxically enough – a convergent path and, for that reason, I will consider them here as a whole.

34 Thomas Elsaesser, 'Louis Lumière – the cinema's first virtualist', in *Cinema Futures: Cain, Abel or Cable? The Screen Arts in the Digital Age*, ed. Thomas Elsaesser and Kay Hoffmann (Amsterdam: Amsterdam University Press, 1998).

35 William Rothman, 'The Filmmaker as Hunter: Robert Flaherty's *Nanook of the North*', in *Documenting the Documentary: close readings of documentary film and video*, ed. Barry Keith Grant and Jeannette Sloniowski (Detroit: Wayne State University Press, 1998).

36 Bill Nichols, *Representing Reality: issues and concepts in documentary* (Bloomington: Indiana University Press, 1991) and Michael Renov, *Theorizing Documentary* (New York: Routledge, 1993).

37 Timothy Murray, 'By way of introduction: digitality and the memory of cinema, or, bearing the losses of the digital code', *Wide Angle* 21, 1 (1999): 6.

38 See Chapter 1, n. 19.

39 Carl Plantinga, 'Moving Pictures and the Rhetoric of Nonfiction Film: Two Approaches', in *Post-Theory: Reconstructing Film Studies*, ed. David Bordwell and Noël Carroll (Madison: University of Wisconsin Press, 1996), 321.

40 Thomas Elsaesser, 'Digital Cinema: delivery, event, time', in *Cinema Futures: Cain, Abel or Cable? The Screen Arts in the Digital Age*, ed. Thomas Elsaesser and Kay Hoffmann (Amsterdam: Amsterdam University Press, 1998), 208.

41 Thomas Elsaesser, 'Between Style and Ideology', *Monogram* 3 (1972): 4.

42 Andrew, *Concepts in Film Theory*, 50.

43 Warren Buckland, 'Between science fact and fiction: Spielberg's digital dinosaurs, possible worlds, and the new aesthetic realism', *Screen* 40, 2 (1999): 134.

44 Manovich, *The Language of New Media*, 301.

45 Buckland, 'Between science fact and fiction', 189–90.

46 Philip Rosen calls this process 'digital mimicry'. Philip Rosen, *Change Mummified: Cinema, Historicity, Theory* (Minneapolis: Minnesota University Press, 2001), 309.

47 According to Bolter and Grusin the logic of immediacy has a twin logic, that of hypermediacy. As they note, 'If the logic of immediacy leads one either to erase or to render automatic the act of representation, the logic of hypermediacy

acknowledges multiple acts of representation and makes them visible. Where immediacy suggests a unified visual space, contemporary hypermediacy offers a heterogeneous space, in which representation is conceived of not as a window on to the world, but rather as "windowed" itself with windows that open on to other representations or other media'. Jay David Bolter and Richard Grusin, *Remediation: Understanding New Media* (Cambridge, MA: MIT Press, 1999), 33–4.

48 Steve Neale, 'Questions of genre', in *Film Genre Reader II*, ed. Barry Keith Grant (Texas: University Texas Press, 1995), 160. I will discuss these concepts in more detail in Chapter 4.

49 I will discuss in more detail how Hollywood films have affected news reporting in Chapter 3.

50 Bordwell, Staiger, and Thompson, *The Classical Hollywood Cinema*, 50–5.

51 Thomas Levin, 'Rhetoric of the Temporal Index: Surveillant Narration and the Cinema of "Real Time"', in *CTRL Space: Rhetorics of Surveillance from Bentham to Big Brother*, ed. Thomas Levin, Ursula Frohne, and Peter Weibel (Karlsruhe: Center for Art and Media, 2002), 585.

52 The phatic function entails the establishment and maintenance of the contact between two poles of communication but not the exchange of ideas or information. Roman Jakobson, 'Closing statements: Linguistics and Poetics', in *Style in language*, ed. T. A. Sebeok (Cambridge, MA: MIT Press, 1960).

53 Mary Ann Doane, 'Information, Crisis, Catastrophe', in *Logics of Television: Essays in Cultural Criticism*, ed. Patricia Mellencamp (Bloomington: Indiana University Press, 1990), 225.

54 Jérôme Bourdon, 'Live television is still alive: on television as an unfulfilled promise', *Media Culture Society* 22 (2000): 538.

55 Arild Fetveit describes most aptly this paradox when he talks about the 'unresolvable tension between the illustrative and the evidential, the iconic and the indexical'. Arild Fetveit, 'Reality TV in the digital era: a paradox in visual culture?', *Media Culture Society* 21 (1999): 792.

56 In Paul Rabinow, *The Foucault reader* (London: Penguin Books, 1991), 73.

57 The role of this tagline ('a comedy about truth, justice and other special effects') is also discussed in Chapters 1 and 3.

58 Jay David Bolter, 'The Desire for Transparency in an Era of Hybridity', *Leonardo* 39, 2 (2006).

59 Gerard Gaylard, 'The Postmodern archaic: the return of the real in digital virtuality', Postmodern *Culture* 15, 1 (2004), 2008, http://muse.jhu.edu/journals/postmodern_culture/v015/15.1gaylard.html [Accessed 8 April 2008].

60 For more on human agency, see Chapter 4.

3

Wag the Dog and the Media

Introduction

In this chapter, I will continue to investigate the relation of film and reality but no longer from a formal and modal point of view, as in the previous two chapters. Instead, I will switch my focus from the filmic text to the afilmic reality in order to examine the historical and political context in which *Wag the Dog* was produced. Then I will engage with what Souriau would call the 'spectatorial events', discussing the ways in which the screening of the film affected the way people would interpret the American political reality for years to come. I will argue that Levinson's film inadvertently became an emblematic case study for the evolving relation between fiction and reality in contemporary media-saturated society, urging us to reconsider some of our longstanding assumptions about art imitating or revealing reality.

There was nothing in the pre-production or filming stage of *Wag the Dog* that could foretell its fated trajectory. It was originally a small project that was squeezed into Levinson's agenda while filming the big budget *Sphere*. Despite the star cast, featuring De Niro and Hoffman in the leading roles, its independent status combined with a political theme traditionally considered as box office poison were most likely to ensure a moderate exposure to the wide audience. Indeed, *Wag the Dog*'s wide release on 9 January 1998 would have seemed rather uneventful, if a few days later, on 21 January *The Washington Post* had not officially reported the outbreak of the Lewinsky scandal.[1] The eerie coincidence of the film's narrative with the twist in Clinton's presidential career triggered a fervent discussion around the relation between art and life, rising to a crescendo a few months later when the US launched a series of attacks in Sudan and Afghanistan. At that point, the distinction between fact and fiction, or rather real and surreal, in most media reports (newspapers, TV news, soft news, etc.) reached a zero-degree level. As Joseph Hayden, former journalist, observed, '*Wag the Dog* may have provided the most surreal experience in twentieth-century presidential history.'[2] The hype in the media about the film led a considerable number of TV viewers to rush to the video stores and rent a copy in order to follow the references and the parallels that the reporters and analysts were drawing between the actual events and the fictional plot.[3] According to *The Economist*, the makers of *Wag the Dog* were responsible for 'one of the luckiest pieces of timing in screen history' causing the film to become part of cultural semantics; its title would qualify as an adjective next to the words 'scenario', 'syndrome' or 'phenomenon', signifying a particular fictional template of fabricating news and manufacturing consent.[4]

As time passed, the impact of *Wag the Dog* in public discourse grew stronger. Instead of its reputation dying down, as one would expect, the film became a 'media event'[5] and a significant point of reference for diverse strands of research in the humanities and social sciences, as I demonstrated in my introduction. The film's narrative and the surrounding political context entered an unprecedented intertextual relay that unsettled some of the fundamental values of contemporary politics. The contradictions and the tension between what is real and what is not, which I analysed in the previous chapter as part of the diegesis, now leaped into the public sphere, causing the diegetic world to spill over into the real.

In order to understand how *Wag the Dog* became a media event and marked a new era for the relation between cinema and reality, we need to delve into the historical and political events that preceded and followed its making. Thus, I will begin this chapter by discussing three major historical and political developments in the United States, which laid the ground for some of the key narrative points in *Wag the Dog*; first, the 1991 Gulf War, then the role of David Gergen as a prominent communications consultant in the White House and, finally, the Oliver North phenomenon. I will then trace the evolving critical reception of the film at various historical junctures; starting from its initial release to the Lewinsky scandal, the Sudan and Afghanistan bombings, the war in Iraq and through to Barack Obama's campaign for re-election in 2012. The persisting reputation of *Wag the Dog* in the American political scene will lead me to a comparison between high-concept filmmaking and what Deborah Jaramillo calls 'high concept war coverage'.[6] With the help of this analogy and the conceptual frame of the digital as laid out in Chapter 2, I will try to formulate, albeit tentatively, a new way to approach the film/reality binary.

The Gulf War never took place?[7]

The American political scene in the 1990s and, particularly, the Persian Gulf War provided Levinson and his screenwriters with a blueprint for the fictional plot. The Gulf War, waged by a coalition of forces led by the United States, was the first war in world history to break on TV; at least, this is how it registered in the memory of hundreds of millions of viewers around the globe. The American president George Bush was part of the TV audience too. According to the reports, he 'was fiddling with the TV remote control when the bombing was due to start, and showed almost childish delight when the raid on Baghdad came through live on television at the time he had ordered it.'[8]

The TV viewers had a 24-hour live coverage of the war but there was hardly any coverage of the communication campaign launched by the Bush administration to mobilize public opinion for an American invasion in the Middle East. Right from the start, the media supported the government's decision to go to war and became propaganda vehicles, as is usually the case in periods of crisis.[9] Through press conferences and other official or unofficial contacts with the journalists, Bush's officials were spreading news about the crisis, such as Iraq's refusal to negotiate the retreat from Kuwait and its plan to invade Saudi Arabia.[10] All the information coming from government sources was broadcast as news pieces in the media, creating the impression that the United States had no choice but to intervene to stop a brutal dictator. It is indicative to mention that the news channels were inclined to report the government officials' statements as facts, even when concrete evidence suggested otherwise. For example, Bush and Pentagon representatives reported the presence of 80,000–100,000 Iraqi soldiers in Kuwait and another 100,000 on the Saudi Arabian borders. When ABC reporters found satellite photographs of occupied Kuwait from a Soviet agency and they realized that the number of Iraqis did not match the official estimate, they refused to publish them and carried on supporting the government story.[11] But even without the cover up from ABC and other news networks, the US government would still have no trouble convincing the public of its supposed enemies; as former CIA officer Ralph McGehee told journalist Joel Bleifuss, 'There has been no hesitation in the past to use doctored satellite photographs to support the policy position that the US wants supported.'[12]

Apart from the disinformation campaign of the Bush administration, the government of Kuwait and some wealthy members of the royal family paid $10.8 dollars to Hill & Knowlton, an international public relations company, to launch an operation for turning US public opinion and the Congress in favour of the war to liberate Kuwait.[13] The company carried out focus group surveys to detect what stirs fear or anger in the common mind so that they would formulate their messages accordingly.[14] One of their findings was that what scared the Americans the most was the image of Hitler. Thus, Saddam Hussein would be likened to Hitler and the Iraqis to the Nazis.[15] As Douglas Kellner notes, Hill & Knowlton organized a photo exhibition of Iraqi atrocities at the United Nations and the US Congress, which then circulated widely on television. They also assisted Kuwaiti refugees in telling stories of torture, lobbied Congress and prepared video and print material for the media'.[16]

However, the most outrageous piece of propaganda spread by Hill & Knowlton was the story of Nayirah, a girl who tearfully testified to the House of Representatives Human Rights Caucus that she had witnessed Iraqi soldiers remove 15 newborn babies from their incubators and abandon them on the floor of the hospital to die. The witness' identity was not disclosed to protect her family from reprisals. The firm produced a video news release (VNR) of her testimony, which was shown on NBC *Nightly News* and then was distributed to some 700 TV stations to end up being watched as a solid piece of news by an estimated audience of 35 million Americans.[17] Two years later, it was revealed that the girl was, in fact, the daughter of the Kuwaiti Ambassador to the US and she was coached by Hill & Knowlton to fake her confession.[18] By that time, the war was over and media had changed their agenda.

In contrast to the fabricated stories of Hill & Knowlton, which were the staple of the evening news, the anti-war voices were rarely heard during the Gulf War. A survey by Fairness and Accuracy In Reporting (FAIR) group revealed that during the first five months of the crisis, ABC allotted only 0.7 per cent of the Gulf coverage to those who questioned the military operation, while CBS allowed 0.8 per cent of the war news to refer to protests and anti-war organizations. The exclusion of the dissident views becomes even more illustrative in FAIR's report if we look at the actual time that was dedicated to them; from the 2,855 minutes of TV war coverage from 8 August to 3 January, only 29 minutes dealt with popular opposition to the US intervention.[19]

Another issue suppressed by the media but mentioned with an ironical undertone in *Wag the Dog*, was the fact that the Bush administration eschewed once again – just as in North Korea, Vietnam and Latin America – the need to declare war against Iraq. In the film, Brean explains to Fad King that the US has not declared war since World War II, so there is no need to declare war against Albania. All they need to do is simply *go to war*. The significance of this sardonic comment could go unnoticed if one ignored the fact that the American constitution contains two important clauses for the declaration of war, ensuring the respect to democratic procedures in periods of crisis. The first requirement entails the official declaration of war by the Congress, while the second necessitates the consultation of the population implied by the Second Amendment. As Elaine Scarry observes, 'with the loss of these two constitutional safeguards, we have become a kind of military monarchy where the President acts alone and where neither the Congress nor the population has any part in military decisions.'[20]

When the war began, the political and military leadership of the US had already determined most thoroughly the rules for the news and image reports in the media. As Taylor notes, 'war was too serious a business to be left to journalists.'[21] Largely, the newspool system that operated during the war constrained the journalists' initiatives and allowed the military to construct the image of war as it best suited them. FAIR's reports constantly traced examples of news items where the journalists had become, knowingly or not, mouthpieces of the military power adopting its vocabulary in the most uncritical manner.[22]

The military propaganda was also boosted by the video footage accompanying the regular briefings of the US army spokespersons. The images of the Patriot missiles hitting their target became regular items on the journalists' news reports without the latter worrying about the origins or the veracity of that visual material. *Wag the Dog* makes an explicit reference to the very first video of the Gulf War, a bomb travelling down the roof ventilation shaft of a building taken from a Stealth F-117A's laser target designator.[23] In Brean's words: 'The Gulf War? Smart bomb falling down a chimney. Twenty-four hundred missions a day. A hundred days. One video of one bomb, Mr Motss, and the American people bought that war.' The reality of the TV coverage of the Gulf War was not as far from the fiction as one might have thought. According to the television critic of the *Observer*, 'Nobody seemed interested, for example, in knowing whether this dramatic footage was statistically representative of the aerial assault. And, of course, nobody asked whether it was the genuine undoctored article.'[24] Those images reconstructed the Gulf crisis as a unique real-time spectacle full of suspense, and yet without any blood. The sight of the dead and wounded soldiers was highly prohibited and never reached the TV screens. Similarly, the real numbers of the Patriot missiles' successes were not revealed until after the end of the war.[25]

Overall, the presence of 24-hour live TV coverage during the 1991 Gulf War marked a turning point in modern warfare. For the first time, the American public had the opportunity to watch a war broadcast live on television and the impact of that exposure was tremendous. According to the polls, the popularity of President Bush's policy rose to 90 per cent, illustrating how presidential power is strengthened under the pretext of a foreign crisis.[26] The events of the crisis in the Gulf War and the role of the media were highly debated over the years that followed, yielding a considerable amount of literature on the status of warfare in our media-saturated societies. Considering all this, the script of *Wag the Dog* no longer appears to be preposterous; in fact, it seems realistic and even, ironically enough, historically accurate at certain points.

Spin doctoring, foreign enemies and national heroes

Apart from the war, *Wag the Dog* provides a very carefully crafted profile of the president's spin-doctor incarnated in Brean's character. The role of 'Mr Fix-it', as Ames calls him, is to handle the communication crisis caused by the scandal at any cost. Brean's spin actions might seem exaggerated but, again, a comparison with the real facts will prove otherwise. Handling the news, co-operating with the journalists and keeping good public relations are essential for almost any kind of political activity, let alone running the White House. Richard Nixon inaugurated the White House Office of Communications in 1969 but the glory days came with David Gergen as Director of Communications for Reagan. Gergen was characterized as 'Spinmeister' and the 'Sultan of spin' by journalists for elevating Reagan's popularity and promoting him as a leader of 'unique gifts and moral standing'.[27] Gergen's work owed its impressive results to a methodical and systematic communication policy, which included some of the following steps:[28]

1. Weekly meetings for the long-range communication strategy and the long-term news agenda.
2. Daily meetings of the communication team to determine what they wanted the press to cover and how.[29]
3. Repetition of the same message with minimum superficial changes. As a key team member, Mike Deaver, remembers: 'It used to drive the President crazy, because repetition was so important. He'd get on that airplane and

look at that speech and say "Mike, I'm not going to give this same speech about education, am I?" I said, "Yeah, trust me, it's going to work". And it did.'[30]

4. Tight and constant control of the press by providing regular and pre-packaged news feed. According to Leslie Janka, a press officer who worked in both Nixon and Reagan administrations, 'They [journalists] have got to write their story every day. You give them their story, they'll go away. As long as you come in there every day, hand them a well-packaged, premasticated story in the format they want, they'll go away. The phrase is "manipulation by inundation". You give them the line of the day, you give them press briefings, you give them facts, access to people who will speak on the record.... And you do that long enough, they're going to stop bringing their own stories, and stop being investigative reporters of any kind, even modestly so.'[31]

5. Regular polls and market research into all kinds of areas to get a grasp of how the public thinks and how the president could affect them through the news. With the famous pollster Richard Wirthlin on the team, the communication office could constantly map the sways of public opinion and control the news accordingly.

The compliance to these communication rules, among others, ensured Reagan a particularly popular presidency. On the contrary, whenever one chose to defy them, their popularity polls soon hit the ground. This was the case of Bill Clinton when he first took office; he considered it unnecessary or even degrading to follow the rules of press manipulation and he cut off the ties between the White House communication personnel and the journalists. Soon afterwards the journalists waged war against him and started attacking his personal life to the extent that Meg Greenfield, the editorial page editor of the *Washington Post*, said that she had seen a lot of harsh media criticism of presidents in her 28 years in Washington journalism, but never had she seen an administration 'pronounced dead so early.'[32]

One of Clinton's weak spots was his promiscuous behaviour towards members of the opposite sex, a recurrent theme in American presidential history, which also inspired the key plotline in *Wag the Dog*. After John F. Kennedy's extramarital affairs were revealed in the 1970s, Clinton's reputation was tarnished by regular rumours about his sexual behaviour, dating from the time he was a governor in Arkansas. Particularly during the 1996 presidential campaign, with

Jennifer Flowers and Paula Jones' stories out in the open, the issue of 'character' became one of Bob Dole's arguments against Clinton.[33] The fact that Clinton neglected his communication policy after winning the election made him even more susceptible to media attacks and hostile rumours. The solution came again from Gergen, who was promptly called upon to handle the crisis and reverse the hostile treatment of the president by the media. Indeed, Gergen applied his old methods and improved Clinton's image but he was never allowed the initiative he enjoyed during the Reagan era. According to Bennett, Gergen was often invited to the White House to deal with emergency situations but when the danger was gone he would be once again pushed to the margins of the presidential cycles.[34] As a result, the White House communication policy remained sloppy and unstable and Clinton faced regular problems with the press that put his political career in danger.

The emphasis placed on the power of communication in *Wag the Dog* appears to be entirely justified when we look at what happens in real politics. It turns out that what determines a successful presidency is not the political actions but the way they are presented to the public. *Wag the Dog*'s rhetoric is also justified on two other counts, namely the strategic use of the concept of 'national security' and of the 'war hero'. As far as national security is concerned, it is very enlightening to look at the argument of prominent political scientist Murray Edelman, who notes,

> One of the most frequent and most prominent evocative terms in political discussion is 'national security', a symbol that generates fear of the enemies of the states. The division of the world's peoples into disparate nationalities inevitably creates fears that other nations might act in a hostile way; so there is always a ready audience for concerns about 'national security'. […] It remains a paramount issue regardless of whether conditions actually support or justify any ground for concern.[35]

Communication consultants have often taken advantage of the concerns for national security and have often magnified or even constructed the threat of foreign enemies in order to divert public attention from domestic controversies. Edelman described the process of construction and the usage of enemies in his book *Constructing the Political Spectacle* (1988), where he claims that the hostility against a foreign country is grounded on a narrative about the past and the future, rationalizing the intervention of the United States and justifying the measures to eradicate the evil.[36] Remember how Brean justified his choice of Albania as the enemy; Ames asked him what Albania ever did to us and he replied saying, 'What have they ever done *for* us?' The need for a story with a beginning, middle and end in order to make sure the public understands the conflict in an unequivocal manner is remarkably similar in fiction and reality. Edelman is also insightful about another element that is particularly emphasized in the film, namely the speed and the effectiveness of a war threat. In his words, 'national security is a symbol-key, as the fear of a foreign attack is a contagious disease spreading rapidly'.[37]

Another cornerstone of American mythology is the national hero. The story of Oliver North is an emblematic example in the history of American politics that rivals in absurdity *Wag the Dog*'s Sergeant William Schumann. Oliver North was a Lieutenant Colonel in the US Marine force, who was one of the key players in the Iran/Contra scandal in 1987 during Reagan's presidency. North and other Reagan associates were revealed to have sold weapons to Iran in exchange of American hostages who were supposedly kept by terrorist groups in the Middle East. The profits from the weapons were laundered in Swiss banks and then supplied to Contras for their guerrilla war in Nicaragua. These actions violated the Congress rule against supporting the Contras and embroidered the president and other prominent officials in a major scandal. Of all the people involved in this affair, the media focused their attention only on North and the personalization of the news once again functioned as a 'convenient substitution for explaining a complicated and deliberately obscure political process.'[38] As North took all the blame, the involvement of the FBI, the CIA and the Pentagon could easily go unheeded.

What is most impressive, however, is how North managed to overthrow the heavy accusations against him and become a national hero. He appeared before Congress as an American patriot who defied the law and bureaucracy to support Contras' fight for freedom. The TV networks, which broadcast his hearings live, compared 'Ollie', as they called him, to Rambo and Dirty Harry. North himself employed the tool of intertextuality to create a favourable impression, saying on one occasion, 'I came … to tell the truth, the good, the bad and the ugly.'[39] What assisted the media in portraying North as a national hero was the fact that he had served in Vietnam. The TV crews went to his hometown and interviewed his friends and neighbours, receiving testimonies of his patriotism and bravery. One of his war companions remarked, 'He's a compassionate man. He's a loyal man. He's patriotic, and he's a marine. I'd follow him to Hell if he'd lead the way 'cause I figure we could get back.'[40] Parallel to these statements other rumors began to surface concerning his feats in Vietnam, which mythologized North but were never true. In the light of Oliver North's story, *Wag the Dog*'s take on heroic patriotism seems more justified. The plot twist of an ex-convict turned hero resonates with North's illegal past while the rhetoric of the war hero campaign echoes the slogans and catchphrases used by the media in their effort to sell North as a hero.

Overall, a brief overview of a number of key events in the American political life from the 1970s onwards indicated several potential sources of inspiration for the makers of *Wag the Dog*. Despite its fictional status, the story world refers to the historic reality in a more direct manner than an average viewer is able to grasp during a casual viewing. What would catch everybody's attention, however, is how the story would relate to events happening around the time of screening and well after it.

Reviews and media references

Even though the producers of *Wag the Dog* would hardly promote it as a 'historical film', the close ties of *Wag the Dog* with a number of historical facts confirmed most theorists' view that films, knowingly or not,[41] always amount to a document of a past reality. In other words, so far there is nothing exceptional. However, *Wag the Dog* would also become a precursor of a series of *future* developments with its fictional narrative providing an interpretive framework for the real facts that took place soon after its screening.[42] It is precisely at that point when the distance between reality and cinema was short-circuited, rendering it impossible to draw a distinction between what is real and what is not. This temporary collision of fact with fiction is what makes *Wag the Dog* such an invaluable case study for understanding the evolving relationship between cinema and the real world and for conceptualizing the new status of truth in a multiply mediated political reality. A short chronicle of the afilmic events is again essential to clarify this point.

As I previously noted, the Lewinsky scandal broke in the media only days after the wide release of *Wag the Dog* causing inevitable comparisons between reality and fiction. Yet, that was only the beginning. In August 1998, the sex scandal reached its apex, as new evidence proved that Clinton had lied to the American people about his relationship with the former White House intern. On 20 August, when Lewinsky was giving her last deposition with new details about her affair with the president, Clinton ordered the bombing of a pharmaceutical factory in Sudan and of a paramilitary training camp in Afghanistan. The co-ordination of these two events, the deposition and the bombings, triggered suspicion regarding the motivation of the military attacks, and the same suspicion resurfaced once again in December when Clinton ordered the bombing of Iraq on the same day that Congress was going to vote for his impeachment for the sex scandal.

The peculiar resemblance of *Wag the Dog*'s story with the real events mentioned above increased dramatically the impact of the film on American and global public opinion and determined the journalists' stance towards Clinton's actions. Indicatively, from January 1998 to April 1999 the two major American newspapers, *The New York Times* and *The Washington Post*, published 26 and 38 main articles respectively, commenting on the parallel between the film and political developments in the United States. It is worth carving out the trajectory of *Wag the Dog*'s reputation by looking closely at the reviews when it first opened and following the media references to the film from the Lewinsky scandal onwards to this date.

The reviews published directly after the official opening of the film were rather ambivalent. There are those who loved it and those who hated it. There are those who found it remarkably cynical and those who considered it remarkably soft. Almost everyone agreed that it is an entertaining movie, a political satire with a stellar cast and professional filmmaking standards, but *Wag the Dog* was deemed equivocal both regarding the plausibility of its plot and its political message. Starting with the negative reviews, I would like to note *Empire*'s following remark: 'content with its initial premise, the movie lacks the necessary bite to develop the satire further, to the point where it's difficult to spot whether Washington or Hollywood is the target.'[43] Along the same lines, the *CNN showbiz* review notes that *Wag the Dog* 'grabs the satire by the tail,'[44] while *Box Office Magazine* lists a number of things that went wrong with the movie to conclude that 'unfortunately, this "Dog" is almost all bark and almost no bite.'[45] According to Gary Johnson, the reviewer of *Images*, '*Wag the Dog* overflows with cynicism of a particularly nasty variety. [...] *Wag the Dog* runs out of steam at about the halfway point and then drifts aimlessly toward its conclusion.'[46] Oddly enough, on the other side of the Atlantic the reviews noted just the opposite; for instance, the Parisian newspaper *Le Monde* found the film too mellow to be subversive. It acknowledges the witty dialogues while it argues that Levinson turned Larry Beinhart's novel into a fairytale. According to the review: '*Wag the Dog* is not a subversive film, as we had the right to expect, but the prank of a good student who would immediately apologize to his professor for having shown disrespect'[47] [my translation from French].

The positive reviews, on the other hand, initially focused on David Mamet and Hilary Henkin's witty writing. On 22 December 1997, the *Newsweek* reviewer, David Ansen, characterized *Wag the Dog* as 'the most wickedly entertaining movie of the season', arguing that 'it's a deliciously outrageous premise, and director Barry Levinson and writers David Mamet and Hilary Henkin know just how to spin it, savaging Washington and Hollywood with merciless wit.'[48] In the same vein, Kenneth Turan from the *Los Angeles Times* wrote: 'a gloriously cynical black comedy that functions as a wicked smart satire on the interlocking worlds of politics and show business, *Wag the Dog* confirms every awful thought you've ever had about media manipulation and the gullibility of the American public.'[49] Ansen and Turan spoke of the Hollywood and Washington connection merely by referring to *Wag the Dog*'s plot, while the reviewer of *The Sunday Times* a few months later went deeper into the film's implications, noting that:

> While you watch *Wag the Dog*, you spend a lot of time laughing. But afterwards you spend a lot of time thinking – and when you stop thinking, you don't feel like laughing anymore. [...] The film constantly refers to recent history, so you are left wondering if you will ever again believe any government report (...)[50]

The concerns about *Wag the Dog*'s political message became even more serious as the real events surrounding Clinton's presidency seemed to emulate to an alarming degree those that took place within the film's diegesis. From the first moment that the Lewinsky scandal broke, the newspapers in the United States and Europe rushed to underscore the eerie similarity of that story with *Wag the Dog*'s key premise. The connection between the two 'stories' hailed immediately by the journalists contributed to a growing interest in the film, while its key players were asked to comment on the fascinating coincidence. Levinson wrote an article in *Newsweek* stating among other things that

> When we were making the movie, we were intrigued by the players (the media and the politicians) in a culture in which the lines between Hollywood and Washington and news and entertainment are rapidly blurring. And in a way, the line between fact and fiction may be getting fuzzy too.[51]

Satisfied with *Wag the Dog*'s insightfulness, Dustin Hoffman said, 'I look at the news these days as if it's a new movie like ours, but a more outrageous scenario. It looks like fiction to me. It doesn't look like real news. It lays itself out like rushes from a movie.'[52] Finally, Mamet made the most intuitive comment of all, saying 'My secret psychotic fantasy is that someone in the White House is saying, "What we should do is go to war, but we can't even do it because of that movie".'[53]

Newspapers and magazines made regular references to *Wag the Dog* in order to comment on Clinton's sex scandal and ventured various comparisons between reality and fiction. For instance, in an article called 'Wag the Clinton', the writers of *Time* drew several parallels between the movie and real life to conclude that 'a comparison reveals that Tinseltown fantasy is far tamer than inside-the-Beltway reality.'[54] In the same issue, another article on the topic entitled 'The Reckless and the Stupid' argues that,

> What Clinton needs now is a producer like the one played by Dustin Hoffman in the movie *Wag the Dog*, a man who, when confronted with a hideously impossible public relations problem like the one facing Clinton, announces bouncily, 'This is NOTHING!'[55]

Many commentaries on the correlation between the film and the Lewinsky scandal are found in the *Washington Post*.[56] On the first day of the revelation, Richard Cohen opened his article as follows: 'It may be time to bomb Albania',[57] while three days later another *Post* writer observes,

> The empire of reality strikes back. We're in the middle of an eerie interplay between pulp fiction and pulp life: A movie arrives claiming to be satiric in its depiction of spin masters trying to wrestle a Washington scandal to the mat. Three weeks later, along comes the real thing – bigger, crazier, stranger, funnier and possibly more tragic than anything any filmmaker could come up with.[58]

In parallel with the sex scandal, the White House started building up tension in the relations with Iraq threatening to launch a 'Desert Thunder' operation against Saddam Hussein. Already in February 1998, *Le Monde* dedicated two articles to the discussion of *Wag the Dog*, the threats against Iraq and the collision of reality with fiction.[59] One of the commentators noted that the Iraqi television urgently broadcast Levinson's film as they awaited Clinton's attack.[60] At that point, not only did fiction forestall reality, but it was also used in turn as a tool to affect and, in this case, avert reality. Yet, reality would not stop emulating fiction even then. In fact, their interplay would continue most consistently for months to come; after the first part of the filmic plot – the sex scandal – materialized in real life, the fear for the materialization of the second part – the war – came true only a few months later.

On 20 August 1998, three days after admitting his 'inappropriate relationship' with Lewinsky on national television, Clinton ordered strikes on suspected terrorist facilities in Sudan and Afghanistan, spreading suspicion around the motives of his decision. As the correspondent of *Le Monde* in New York observed, 'it didn't take more than half an hour after Mr Clinton's announcement for the "*Wag the Dog* syndrome" to take over Washington and spread into the press rooms.'[61] *Wag the Dog* was repeatedly mentioned in news reports across all media while numerous politicians were asked to comment on the similarities of Clinton's actions and the movie. One of the first questions addressed to Defense Secretary William Cohen in a nationally-televised press conference from the Pentagon, was how he would respond to people who think the military action 'bears a striking resemblance to *Wag the Dog*'. His response seemed to come right out of Motss' lips: 'The only motivation driving this action today was our absolute obligation to protect the American people from terrorist activities.'[62] Other politicians in Washington questioned the timing of the attacks and some of them even made direct references to the movie. For instance, a member of the Congress, Jim Gibbons, stated: 'Look at the movie *Wag the Dog*. I think it has all the elements of that movie. Our reaction to the embassy bombings should be based on credible evidence, not a knee-jerk reaction to try to direct public attention away from his personal problems.'[63]

The vast majority of the press made regular references to the film regardless of their stance towards Clinton's actions. The *New York Times* published eight main articles commenting on the relation between the film and reality. Similarly, between 21 and 31 August 1998, the *Washington Post* published 11 relevant pieces with titles such as 'In the midst of the scandal, Clinton planned action', 'For President Clinton, a change of subject', or 'Life is not a movie, is it?'[64] Furthermore, extensive research into the references to *Wag the Dog* in soft and hard TV news programmes using Lexis-Nexis clearly shows how the American nation employed the film as a 'frame'[65] for understanding governmental decisions. As Matthew Baum writes,

> I found that, in the week following the attacks, 35 of 46 soft news stories on the subject (or 76%) addressed the *Wag the Dog* theme, repeatedly raising the question of whether the President might have launched the missile strikes to distract the nation from the Lewinsky scandal. In contrast, during that same period, the three network evening news programs, combined, mentioned *Wag the Dog* or Monica Lewinsky in only 11 of 69 (16%) stories on the missile strikes.[66]

Even though Baum emphasizes that soft news programmes discussed the film far more, it is remarkable that *Wag the Dog* even made it into 16 per cent of the evening news stories seven months after its screening. As far as the foreign coverage of the attacks is concerned, a survey conducted by the Department of State using 45 reports from 28 countries on 20–21 August shows how the president's credibility had been damaged by *Wag the Dog*'s use as a frame. The extensive comparisons with the film made it difficult for the president to dispel the suspicion that he was trying to deflect public attention from his personal troubles.[67] This was clearly a case of fiction standing in the way of reality.

But what about the truth? Did Clinton launch the missile attacks to change the subject? In all likelihood, Motss' answer would be most apt: 'how the fuck do we know?' The evidence that surfaced a few months after the bombings indicated that the decision was undoubtedly a rushed one. Seymour Hersh's article in the *New Yorker* on 12 October 1998 revealed that the four service officers on the Joint Chiefs of Staff had been deliberately kept in the dark about the Sudan and Afghanistan attacks to bypass their objections.[68] In addition, the Al Shifa pharmaceutical plant in Sudan, which was attacked for supposedly producing chemical weapons, was in fact involved in the processing and marketing of antibiotics and other beneficial drugs, as Sudan proved after the bombing. Similarly, the 'terrorist training camps' targeted in Afghanistan proved to be camps used by Pakistani intelligence officers to equip guerrillas for Kashmir. Thus, the destruction of those sites not only did not eliminate any terrorist threats, but also strained the relations of the United States with Sudan and Pakistan respectively.[69]

Yet, the '*Wag the Dog*' year was still not over. In December 1998, Clinton ordered a three-day bombing of Iraq when Congress was going to decide about his impeachment for the Lewinsky scandal. The crisis in US–Iraq relations had been lurking for a year, as I previously mentioned, but Clinton had not taken any action. His decision to launch the Desert Fox operation against Iraq on the eve of the House impeachment debate triggered once again the *Wag the Dog* comparisons and vindicated the voices, like those expressed in *Le Monde*, which had seen that coming. Compared to the timing of the Afghanistan and Sudan strikes, the timing of the Desert Fox strikes in Iraq could not be too suspicious.[70] The *Washington Post* commented on the change of the media agenda as follows:

> The morning began on television with President Clinton on the verge of impeachment. By noon, that drama was eclipsed by an unscheduled rerun

of 'Showdown With Saddam', and by 5 p.m. the first explosions were shaking Baghdad – all of which left journalists scrambling on two fast-moving fronts.[71]

On a similar note, the *New York Times* wrote,

> 'We interrupt this impeachment to bring you the bombing of Iraq...' What to think? An international crisis in the nick of time? The latest development in a yearlong series of cynical and irresponsible acts by government officials? A President and a Congress locked in a domestic war that has flamed dangerously out of control? Stay tuned.[72]

Clinton's justifications regarding the particular timing were not considered convincing, as various pieces in the press began to cast serious doubts about the true objectives of this military operation.[73] By that time, *Wag the Dog* was already established as a key concept in politics for interpreting presidential decisions. For the other nations, the film became a political tool whenever they faced a threat from the US; both Iraqi and Serbian television aired *Wag the Dog* to supposedly expose the motivations behind the US attacks in Iraq and Kosovo respectively. For the Americans, it became an interpretive tool for evaluating official responses to terrorism, enhancing suspicion 'that any kind of military response was an attempt to generate public support, or even to distract attention from internal crises.'[74] The interference of this film with the news coverage of American foreign policy continued through the years, extending over to key events such as the 9/11 attacks, the war in Iraq in 2003[75] and even, most recently, Barack Obama's re-election campaign in 2012. After a disappointing performance in the first TV debate against Mitt Romney, Obama saw his percentages in the polls dwindle. It was then that a commentator in the *Boston Herald* wrote: 'Is it time to bomb Libya? If ever Barack Obama needed a "Wag the Dog" moment, this is it.'[76] The persisting reputation of *Wag the Dog* in American political culture indicates how the film managed to touch a sensitive chord, especially in the media world, inviting the Americans to return to it over and over again for a 'reality check'. As journalist Andrew Christie had observed already back in 2003, *Wag the Dog* 'is becoming our national portrait in the attic, worth a trip up the stairs every few years so that we may gaze upon its shifting surface and behold the latest, ghastly truths that have become visible there, reflecting our real political face.'[77] Never before, I believe, did fiction bring people face to face with reality in such an upfront manner.

High-concept filmmaking/high-concept wars

The case of *Wag the Dog* is enlightening for exploring the evolving relationship between reality and fiction in contemporary society. On the one hand, the film's diegesis was built on the assumption that the distinction between the real and the fictional is problematic. On the other, however, the creators of the film could not anticipate how this problematic distinction would take on an extratextual life of its own affecting the course of a number of political developments across the globe. The fusion of fact and fiction portrayed in the plot and the materialization of that fusion in the realm of the afilmic bears wider implications for both cinema and society. These implications become even more palpable, if we approach the fact/fiction binary with the help of Deborah Jaramillo's notion of 'high-concept war coverage', which brings cinema and the news closer in yet another way.[78]

High-concept filmmaking is a term coined by Justin Wyatt to designate a strand of Hollywood films from the 1970s onwards that were designed according to certain marketing values.[79] Even though all Hollywood movies are meant to generate profits for the studios, high-concept films are the epitome of a new phase in the history of the entertainment industry characterized by media conglomeration, synergies and the rising of marketing strategies. A high-concept film presents a simple story that can be easily pitched to a wide audience and can lend itself to wide-scale marketing and merchandizing tie-ins. In Wyatt's words, a high-concept film must have 'the look, the hook and the book'.[80] The key ingredients of the high-concept formula include stars, character types, genres, simple narratives, music and a particular style of production design and cinematography. All these elements increase the marketability of the film using familiarity (well-known faces and plots) and simplicity (easily communicated messages). Despite the misleading connotations of 'high', high-concept films in fact rely on easily digestible ideas that have been successfully tried out before. Critics of this trend have pointed out that 'high' is actually a 'misnomer' since the concept is so 'low' that it can be summarized and sold on the basis of a single sentence.[81] Low as the concept may be, the marketing and production tactics are fairly complex and multifarious, as they simultaneously position the stars, the plots, the music and the look in a diegetic as well as an extradiegetic world that engages the audiences not only during their fictional travels in the movie theatre, but in other real life activities as well. This all-encompassing approach to filmmaking has led cinema to interact with reality on multiple levels, blurring the boundaries of the two realms even further.

Deborah Jaramillo takes an interest in high-concept cinema for the way it applies to the production and social function of television news.[82] Despite the obvious discrepancies between the movie-making business and the news media, Jaramillo ventures on a close and systematic analysis of the war coverage of the 2003 US invasion of Iraq in order to detect how the principles of high-concept films influence the form and the content of the war coverage. One of the cornerstones of war reporting is the construction of a war narrative with a simple and clear cause-and-effect logic. The invasion in Iraq was presented as a tale of revenge; after the 9/11 attacks the US declared a war on terror. When CIA reported the existence of weapons of mass destruction in Iraq, they left the Bush administration no choice but to invade the country and eliminate the threat. By taking out Hussein and liberating the Iraqi people, the Americans would protect themselves from a potential terrorist attack. This simplified storyline dominated the war reports and mediated the events to the public in a coherent and solid manner. And whenever any contradictions arose, the media were eager to smooth the rough edges. As Jaramillo points out, 'in constructing the 2003 war as a high-concept narrative, CNN and Fox News Channel encountered holes in the plot and contradictions in the details. When this happened, they chose to massage their analysis of evidence to make it fit their narrative.'[83]

Another high-concept tool embraced by the war coverage was the use of intertextual references. Intertextuality has played a rich and invigorating role in the history of art, but the way it functions within high-concept filmmaking is rather simplistic; it draws on the audience's vast knowledge of media artifacts in order to communicate information quickly and effortlessly. Along the same lines, media reporters conveniently rely on a well-known depository of images, sounds, characters, genres or even lines of dialogue in order to serve the simplicity of the overarching narrative. During the first days of the US invasion, the war reports frequently referred to three key source categories: previous conflicts in the American history, such as the Vietnam War and the 1991 Gulf War, film genres, such as the war film and the western, and movie stars like John Wayne and Bruce Willis.[84]

Moreover, the plainness of the war narrative is grounded on the few stereotyped characters that inhabit it. The formulaic approach to the people involved in the war conflict serves both an economic and an ideological function; the character types are easy to market and they are easy to identify with. By explaining a complex military process in terms of a Manichean struggle between a villain and a hero, the news reports facilitate the audience to understand the conflict and take a clear position towards it. Vilifying Saddam was a well-known strategy from the previous Gulf war, which was then reprised in 2003. Among the heroic figures, on the other hand, the case of Jessica Lynch clearly stands out.[85] The rescue of Private Lynch after she had been captured by Iraqi soldiers supplied the news media with a sensational story. Being the first woman soldier in American history to be rescued by the special operation forces, Lynch qualified both as a female Rambo and a rape victim tortured at the hands of the Iraqis. In fact, her amnesia after the rescue allowed the media enough time to spread her epic tale and generate public enthusiasm. Much to everybody's disappointment, Lynch herself denied the title of heroine, explaining that she never fought back the enemy nor was she ever abused by the Iraqis. Even though the initial version of her adventure began to crumble by mid-May 2003,[86] the media networks were not prevented from exploiting the heroic account in a made-for-TV movie called *Saving Jessica Lynch*, which aired on NBC in November 2003. In this case, the echoes of American patriotism portrayed in *Saving Private Ryan* (1998) proved stronger than the dire warnings of *Wag the Dog*. Instead of *Wag the Dog*'s satire neutralizing the Jessica Lynch story on the evening news, Jessica Lynch's adventure turned into a television biopic and wiped out the irony of Levinson's film, especially its 'rescued soldier device'.[87] Finally, the production of such a TV movie based on a news story brings out another aspect of high-concept war coverage, namely the role of commodification, synergy and merchandizing tie-ins. Jaramillo is careful to underline that an exact parallel between high-concept films and news reports is not easy to draw but the common ground is once again substantial. Even though war reporting is not the output of a centrally planned campaign, the TV news, like films, is also constructed around a central concept or, in Wyatt's words, 'a hook'. According to Jaramillo, 'the marketable concept of the 2003 invasion was the execution of vengeance through technological and moral superiority'.[88] This concept shaped the look and the sounds of the promos of the war reports featuring marching soldiers, Bush officials and embedded reporters. The major TV networks also circulated other promotional material such as video and books chronicles of the invasion. The motifs of the war broadcast on TV soon inspired a series of ancillary tie-ins, such as toys, video-games and even a soundtrack with four songs.[89] Thus, the American invasion was mediated to the public through a series of media products who could no longer be strictly classified either as information or entertainment.

This collapse of distinction between the real and the fictional in high-concept war coverage is precisely what the characters in *Wag the Dog* try to take advantage of. The concoction of the fake war against Albania is facilitated immensely by the tools of high-concept and that is why a Hollywood producer is the most suitable person for this job. When Brean tries to convince Motss to help him 'produce' the war, he says: 'it's a pageant. We need a theme, a song, some visuals. It's a pageant. It's just like the Oscars. That's why we came to you.' The practices of show business quickly take over the planning of the Albanian war, as Motss invites a number of collaborators from Hollywood to assist him in the production. The preparation of the news footage with the Albanian girl, which I have extensively discussed, is the main priority of the team but they simultaneously work on the concept of the war (Terror comes from the North), which will generate ideas about music and other tie-ins, such as armbands and hats. The choice of Albania as the enemy causes them several difficulties because it is a small and unknown country whose culture is not easy to market. For instance, they wonder whether there is a national cuisine or if they can find any famous Albanian people who could function as intermediaries in communicating the conflict to the wide public. When Motss says that James Belushi is Albanian, everybody instantly cheers up and becomes more engaged. But the lack of inspiration tied to Albania persists even to the last minute when Fad King suggests to Brean to use Italy instead. He says: 'I can get my hands on a lot of walking-around-cash if it's Italy. Listen to this concept: the boot. Giv' em the Boot. What if the shoe is the fad?'

The shoe would, in fact, become a fad when the war hero would enter the picture. The Albanian war, like any high-concept narrative, was premised on a clear cause-and-effect logic and, of course, it would be impossible to sustain without the standard war characters.[90] *Wag the Dog* puts its emphasis on the figure of the national hero, a soldier called William Schumann of the 303 Squad who is left behind enemy lines. This plot device is particularly accommodating for a long series of marketing stunts that increase the president's popularity and raise the patriotic spirit in the American people. Brean circulates a photograph of Schumann held in captivity by a dissident group of Albanian terrorists. The journalists notice that his sweater has been unravelled in places to form dashes and dots in the Morse code. The message that Schumann thus tries to communicate is 'Courage Mom'. This message inspires a song by the same title, while another one called 'Old Shoe' is 'rediscovered' and becomes a hit on the charts. The truth was that Johnny Dean, Motss' hired country musician, writes the song

'Old Shoe' to resonate with the soldier's last name and then he digitally inserts a hiss on the track to make it sound old and scratchy. A copy of the supposedly original LP is then implanted into the 1930s folksong collection of the Library of Congress and thus another fabrication passes off as reality. Moreover, T-shirts with slogans like 'Fuck Albania' and 'Save Shoe' become popular, while Burger King introduce a new hamburger called Shoe Burger with 303 sauce.

Apart from the elaborate and widespread marketing campaign of the Albanian crisis, *Wag the Dog* portrays another aspect of social participation in the drama of war, which is often the result of astroturfing. Astroturfing is a relatively new type of political, advertising or public relations campaign, which is meticulously designed to appear as spontaneous and popular grassroots behaviour.[91] In contrast to traditional communication campaigns, which are openly guided by a public entity, such as a political party or a corporate company, astroturfing provokes a public reaction to an event, as if it were independent and naturally occurring. In *Wag the Dog* Brean and Motss initiate the trend of throwing old shoes on trees and lampposts as a symbolic support for the return of Schumann. This carefully implanted idea of participating in a national effort by means of shoe-throwing gathers momentum and the streets are quickly filled with old shoes hanging everywhere. As they walk through a hotel lounge, Brean and Motss glance at a TV news report that shows young students throwing their shoes into a basketball court after the end of the game and yelling 'Bring back Shoe'. The commentator describes this as 'a spontaneous moment of sheer patriotism', and Motss says laughingly 'there is no business like this.'

Conclusion

The afterlife of *Wag the Dog* in the public sphere transformed a low-key independent production into a media event that would occupy the news reports as well as the academic fields of the humanities and social sciences for years to come. For film theorists, in particular, the contribution of this film to our understanding of the relationship of film and reality in the contemporary world is of immense importance. Even though film and reality have always had a complex relationship, the case of *Wag the Dog* shows how this relationship enters a new phase where concepts like imitation, mirroring, or influence are found wanting. The contextualization of this filmic text within an existing historical background and the analysis of the afilmic events after its release indicate a series of changes in the way cinema and the real world interact with each other in the current day and age. More specifically, *Wag the Dog* carefully embedded a series of tropes of American politics from the Reagan administration onwards, such as the communication strategies of the White House and the foreign policy rhetoric in the United States. Moreover, the film's characters openly alluded to the war sensibility established during the Persian Gulf War and made oblique references to a number of fabrications that passed off as reality at the time. The coincidence of the film's release with Clinton's sex scandal reversed the flow of influence, and it was then *Wag the Dog*'s turn to dictate a frame for evaluating and interpreting the President's military actions. The blurring roles of fact and fiction encapsulated in the (hi)story of *Wag the Dog* could be further investigated in the parallel between high-concept filmmaking and high-concept war coverage. The use of 'high-concept' in war coverage, as argued by Jaramillo and as equally portrayed in the film, illustrates how reality purposefully borrows the formulas of fiction to an unprecedented degree. This irrevocable infiltration of fiction in the contemporary regime of truth, to remember Foucault once more,[92] requires a new set of tools and concepts to gauge its significance. One of these tools could be the digital itself. More specifically, I would like to argue that this new stage in the film/reality binary could be approached with the aid of the digital *as a guiding metaphor*. In other words, the conceptual framework of the digital, as I laid it out in the previous chapter, could be applied in the broader relationship of film and reality and elucidate the dynamics that these two poles have developed.

If we keep the analogy of the digital in mind, the *Wag the Dog* event becomes emblematic of the two key operations of the digital, namely the process of negation and the transformation of all data sources to a single numerical code. These two operations were doubly articulated, first at the level of the diegesis, and then at the interaction of the filmic text with the unfolding reality. Let me explain. *Wag the Dog*'s central narrative premise was that you could fabricate a 100 per cent fake war and make it pass off as reality. The story demonstrated the distinctive ability of the digital to simulate something that does not exist, thus performing what Kittler calls a 'negation'.[93] At the same time, the film persistently promoted the idea that you can never know whether something really existed or not, eliminating the distinction between fact and fiction. Technically, this is the distinction also eliminated by the digital platform once it incorporates analogue signs.

Similarly, when we move to the interplay of the film with reality, the distinction between the film scenario and political developments in the domestic and foreign scene cannot be clearly demarcated either. The fictional template was immediately embedded in the way the media and the public received and interpreted the political events, while the film's lasting effect further influenced the political discourse for years to come. The more we look into the specifics of the Clinton affair and the subsequent attacks on foreign targets, the more we realize that it would be impossible to tell where fiction ended and truth began. Just as the digital obliterates distinctions by transforming live-action footage into pixels, the *Wag the Dog* event established that in a media-saturated world telling fact from fiction is no longer attainable. As Elsaesser notes, 'Future generations, looking at the history of the twentieth century, will never be able to tell fact from fiction, having the media as material evidence. But then, will this distinction still matter then?'[94] Therefore, does it matter whether the American attacks in Afghanistan and Sudan were true or whether they were also a negation akin to the Albanian war? *Wag the Dog*, just like Elsaesser, seems to imply that it does not. In this new phase, film and reality are both filtered through the media to become same-order signs with equal mobilizing force. In this sense, the media function just like a computer; they have the capacity to obliterate the origins of information and to simulate either fact or fiction, producing 'truth' merely as a particular type of a 'special effect'. From this perspective, the film's tagline 'a comedy about truth, justice and other special effects' is no longer a joke; it is a very literal conception of the status of truth, and by extension justice, in contemporary society.

The melding of reality and filmic imagination does not end with the case of *Wag the Dog*, however. The collaboration between Washington and Hollywood keeps growing ever stronger. Indicative is the fact that after the 9/11 attacks the military sought help from a number of top Hollywood filmmakers in order to prevent future attacks. As James Der Derian notes,

> In a reversal of roles, government intelligence specialists have been secretly soliciting terrorist scenarios from top Hollywood filmmakers and writers. A unique ad hoc working group convened at USC just last week at the behest of the U.S. Army. The goal was to brainstorm about possible terrorist targets and schemes in America and to offer solutions to those threats, in light of the twin assaults on the Pentagon and the World Trade Center.[95]

Whether Steven De Souza, the writer of *Die Hard* (1981), or David Fincher, the director of *Fight Club* (1999),[96] will be providing the White House with future military targets is certainly something we need to look into for a number of reasons. As far as the study of film is concerned, I believe we need to explore the evolving relation of film and reality with the same sobriety that we need to maintain as we explore the digital itself. We know that certain aspects of it are new, but we are also aware that several others have been with us for quite a while.

Notes

1. Susan Schmidt, Peter Baker, and Toni Locy, 'Clinton Accused of Urging Aide to Lie', *The Washington Post*, January 21, 1998, http://www.washingtonpost.com/wp-srv/politics/special/clinton/stories/clinton012198.htm [Accessed 26 August 2010].
2. Joseph Hayden, *Covering Clinton: The President and the Press in the 1990s* (Westport, CT: Praeger, 2002), 108.
3. Robert Wicks, *Understanding Audiences: Learning To Use the Media Constructively* (New York: Routledge, 2001), 80.
4. 'Is it life or is it Mamet?' *Economist*, 29 January 1998, http://www.economist.com/node/112045 [Accessed 1 May 2013]; James Der Derian, 'Virtually Wagging the Dog', *Theory & Event* 2, no 1 (1998); Joel Black, *The Reality Effect: Film Culture and the Graphic Imperative* (New York, London: Routledge, 2002); Andrew Hoskins, 'Constructing History in TV News from Clinton to 9/11: Flashframes of History-American Visual Memories', in *American Visual Cultures*, ed. David Holloway and John Beck (New York: Continuum Publishing, 2005).
5. A media event is defined as 'an occurrence which attracts an extraordinary amount of media attention. The attention is generally international in scope, crosses the boundaries between popular news and political event, and usually marks a reference point in the cultural and historical imagination thereafter.' Mike Hammond, 'Media Event', in *Critical Dictionary of Film and Television Theory*, ed. Roberta Pearson and Philip Simpson (London and New York: Routledge, 2001), 272.
6. Deborah L. Jaramillo, *Ugly War, Pretty Package: How CNN and Fox News Made the Invasion of Iraq High Concept* (Bloomington: Indiana University Press, 2009).
7. I am borrowing the title from Baudrillard's book *La guerre du Golfe n' a pas eu lieu*. Jean Baudrillard, *La guerre du Golfe n' a pas eu lieu* (Paris: Galilée, 1991).
8. *Independent on Sunday*, 20 January 1991, in Philip, P. Taylor, *War and the Media: Propaganda and Persuasion in the Gulf War* (Manchester: Manchester University Press, 1992), 32.
9. Douglas Kellner, *Media Culture* (London and New York: Routledge, 1995), 198–201.
10. Ibid., 205–6.
11. Ibid., 204–5.
12. Quoted in Ibid., 205.

13 Jarol Manheim, 'Strategic Public Diplomacy: Managing Kuwait's Image During the Gulf Conflict', in *Taken by storm: the media, public opinion, and U.S. foreign policy in the Gulf War*, ed. W. Lance Bennett and David L. Paletz (Chicago: University of Chicago Press, 1994), 138.
14 Kellner, *Media Culture*, 207.
15 Manheim, 'Strategic Public Diplomacy', 131–48.
16 Kellner, *Media Culture*, 207.
17 Lance W. Bennett, *News: the Politics of Illusion* (New York: Longman, 1996), 43.
18 Kellner, *Media Culture*, 207.
19 FAIR, Press Release, January 1991 in Ibid., 209.
20 Elaine Scarry, 'Watching and Authorizing the Gulf War', in *Media Spectacles*, ed. Marjorie Garber, John Matlock, and Rebecca L. Walkowitz (New York, London: Routledge, 1993), 58.
21 Taylor, *War and the Media*, 36.
22 Ibid., 45.
23 Ibid., 46.
24 *Observer*, 20 January 1991 in Ibid., 46.
25 According to Bennett, 'the magnitude of news deception was revealed in a later study by a scientist at the Massachusetts Institute of Technology (MIT), who concluded that the much-heralded missile "may have been an almost total failure to intercept quite primitive attacking missiles".' Bennett, *News: the Politics of Illusion*, 45.
26 Ibid., 44.
27 Ibid., 106; Mark Hertsgaard, *On Bended Knee: The Press and The Reagan Presidency* (New York: Schocken Books, 1989), 344.
28 Hertsgaard, *On Bended Knee*, 32–54.
29 Ibid., 35.
30 Ibid., 49.
31 Ibid., 52.
32 In David Shaw, 'Dire Judgement on Clinton Started Just Days into Term', *Los Angeles Times*, 16 September 1993, http://articles.latimes.com/1993-09-16/news/mn-35815_1_clinton-presidency [Accessed 14 April 2011].
33 Peter Rollins, 'Hollywood's Presidents, 1944–1996: The Primacy of Character', in *Hollywood's White House: The American Presidency in Film and History*, ed. Peter C. Rollins and John E. Connor (Kentucky: Kentucky University Press, 2003), 252.
34 Bennett, *News: the Politics of Illusion*, 170.
35 Murray Edelman, The *Politics of Misinformation* (Cambridge: Cambridge University Press, 2001), 7.
36 Murray Edelman, *Constructing the Political Spectacle* (Chicago: University of Chicago Press, 1988), 75.

37 Ibid., 28.
38 R. Andersen, 'Oliver North and the News', in *Journalism and Popular Culture*, ed. P. Dahlgren and C. Sparks (London: Sage, 1993), 173.
39 Ibid., 187.
40 Ibid., 176.
41 There is extensive literature on the complicated nature of cinema's relation to the historical past and the manifold ways in which a film can function as a historical document. Indicatively, see Marc Ferro, *Cinema and History* (Detroit: Wayne State University Press, 1988) and Robert Rosenstone, *History on film/film on history* (New York: Longman/Pearson, 2006).
42 Richard Maltby, *Hollywood Cinema* (Malden, MA: Blackwell Publishing, 2003), 291.
43 Bob MacCabe, 'Wag the dog', *Empire* 106 (1998), http://www.empireonline.com/site/incinemas/ReviewInFull.asp?FID=3552 [Accessed 30 May 1999]
44 Paul Tatara, '"Wag the Dog" grabs satire by the tail', *CNN*, 6 January 1998, http://edition.cnn.com/SHOWBIZ/9801/06/wag.dog.review/ [Accessed 1 May 2013]
45 Ray Greene, 'Wag The Dog', *Box Office Magazine*, 25 December 1997, http://www.boxofficemagazine.com/reviews/2008-08-wag-the-dog?q=Jane+Rosenthal [Accessed 1 May 2013]
46 Gary Johnson, 'Wag the dog', *Images: A Journal of Film and Popular Culture*, Issue 5, (1998), http://www.imagesjournal.com/issue05/reviews/wag.htm [Accessed 1 May 2013]
47 Samuel Blumenfeld, 'Trop gentil pour être subversif', *Monde*, 30 April 1998.
48 David Ansen, 'Wag the dog', *Newsweek*, 22 December 1997, http://newsweek.com/nw-srv/tnw/today/as/mv/mv_w.htm [Accessed 17 April 2000].
49 Kenneth Turan, 'Wag the Dog Is a Comedy With Some Real Bite to It', *Los Angeles Times*, 24 December 1997, http://articles.latimes.com/1997/dec/24/entertainment/ca-1649 [Accessed 1 May 2013]
50 'So true to life you may have seen the media first', *Sunday Times*, 24 May 1998, www.suntimes.co.za/1998/05/24/arts/ane11.htm [Accessed 24 December 2004]
51 Barry Levinson, 'Hey, we were just kidding', *Newsweek US Edition*, 9 February 1998, http://newsweek.com/nw-srv/issue/06_98a/nw_980209_051_1.htm [Accessed 15 March 1999]
52 In Joey Berlin, 'White House Sex Scandal Cheers Dustin Hoffmann', *Hollywood*, 3 February 2000, www.hollywood.com/news/berlin/02-02-98/ [Accessed 15 March 1999]
53 In Janet Maslin, 'At Sundance, Talk Of Life Imitating Art', *New York Times*, 24 January 1998, http://www.nytimes.com/1998/01/24/movies/critic-s-notebook-at-sundance-talk-of-life-imitating-art.html?pagewanted=all [Accessed 10 January 2012].
54 Kathleen Adams et al., 'Wag the Clinton', *Time Magazine*, Notebook, 151, 4,

2 February 1998, http://www.time.com/time/magazine/article/0,9171,987767,00.html [Accessed 30 May 1999].
55 Lance Morrow, 'The Reckless and the Stupid', *Time Magazine*, 151, 4, 2 February 1998, http://www.time.com/time/magazine/article/0,9171,987761,00.html [Accessed 1 May 2013]
56 In the period from 23 January–19 February 1998 there were seven main articles on the topic.
57 Richard Cohen, 'But is it a matter for the law?' *Washington Post*, 23 January 1998.
58 Stephen Hunter, 'A Tale that Wags the Dog', *Washington Post*, 26 January 1998.
59 Claudine Mulard, 'L' actualité américaine rattrape les films Wag the Dog et Primary Colors', *Monde*, 21 February 1998; Pierre Georges, 'Bande-Annonce', *Monde*, 21 February 1998.
60 Pierre Georges, 'Bande-Annonce'.
61 Sylvie Kauffmann, 'Un répit bienvenu pour un président malmené', *Monde*, 22 February 1998.
62 CNN report at www.cnn.com/ALLPOLITICS/1998/08/21/wag.the.dog/ [Accessed 1 May 2013]
63 CNN report at www.cnn.com/ALLPOLITICS/1998/08/21/wag.the.dog/ [Accessed 1 May 2013]
64 John F. Harris, 'In The Midst of Scandal, Clinton Planned Action', *Washington Post*, 21 August 1998, A1; Tom Shales, *Washington Post*, 21 August 1998, B01; Hunter, 'A Tale that Wags the Dog'.
65 I am using 'frame' according to Gamson and Modigliani's definition, i.e. 'a frame is a central organizing idea or storyline that provides meaning to an unfolding strip of events, weaving a connection among them. The frame suggests what the controversy is about, the essence of the issue.' William A. Gamson and Andre Modigliani, 'The changing culture of affirmative action', *Research in Political Sociology* 3 (1987): 143.
66 Matthew Baum, 'Sex, Lies and War: How soft news brings foreign policy to the inattentive public', *American Political Science Review* 96 (March 2002): 96.
67 Kathleen J. Brahney, 'U.S. Air strikes against Afghanistan, Sudan: Mixed Views on Washington's Action," *USIA*, 21 August 1998, www.usia.gov/admin/005/wwwh8821.html [Accessed 30 May 1999]
68 Seymour M. Hersh, 'Annals of National Security, The Missiles of August', *The New Yorker*, 12 October 1998.
69 Christopher Hitchens, 'Most Dangerous Presidency: weapons of mass distraction', *Vanity Fair*, March 1999.
70 Gene Healy, *The Cult of the Presidency: America's dangerous devotion to executive power* (Washington, DC: Cato Institute, 2008), 127.
71 Howard Kurtz, 'The day the stories snowballed', *Washington Post*, 17 December 1998.

72 Bob Herbert, 'In America; What to think?' *New York Times*, 17 December 1998.
73 The *Washington Post* alone dedicated eight articles to challenging Clinton's justifications.
74 Keith Jenkins, *Images of Terror: What We Can and Can't Know about Terrorism* (New York: Aldine de Gruyter, 2003), 46.
75 The rescue story of Jessica Lynch, an American soldier in Iraq, was repeatedly discussed as another *Wag the Dog* case in American political history. See Carol Mason, 'The Hillbilly defense: culturally mediating US terror at home and abroad', *NWSA Journal*, 17, no 3 (2005) and John Carlos Rowe, 'Culture, US Imperialism, and Globalization', *American Literary History* 16, no 4 (2004).
76 http://www.bostonherald.com/news/columnists/view/20221005obamas_free_ride_over/srvc=home&position=3 [Accessed 1 May 2013]
77 In Robert L. Hilliard, *Hollywood Speaks Out: Pictures that Dared to Protest Real World Issues* (Malden, MA: Wiley-Blackwell, 2009), 168.
78 Jaramillo, *Ugly War, Pretty Package*.
79 Justin Wyatt, *High Concept: Movies and Marketing in Hollywood* (Austin: University of Texas Press, 1994).
80 Ibid., 20.
81 Richard Schickel in Ibid., 13.
82 Jaramillo, *Ugly War, Pretty Package*.
83 Ibid., 84.
84 Ibid., 91–100.
85 Mason, 'The Hillbilly defense'.
86 Jaramillo, *Ugly War, Pretty Package*, 215.
87 Rowe, 'Culture, US Imperialism, and Globalization', 586.
88 Jaramillo, *Ugly War, Pretty Package*, 179.
89 Ibid., 195.
90 I also discuss the plotline of the 'Albanian war' and the function of the characters in Chapter 4.
91 John Stauber and Sheldon Rampton, *Toxic sludge is good for you: lies, damn lies, and the public relations industry* (Monroe, ME: Common Courage Press, 1995).
92 I discussed Foucault's concept of 'regime of truth' in Chapter 2.
93 See Chapter 2.
94 Thomas Elsaesser, 'History Memory Identity and the Moving Image: One Train May be Hiding Another', in *Topologies of Trauma: Essays on the Limit of Knowledge and Memory*, ed. Linda Belau and Petar Ramadanovic (New York: Other Press, 2002), 62.
95 James Der Derian, 'The war of networks', *Theory & Event* 5, 4 (2002).
96 These two names were on the list of the working group at ICT. Ibid.

4

Wag the Dog and Politics in Hollywood

Over the past three generations, the American political movie has been a resilient, frequently neglected but quietly tenacious mirror and shaper, barometer and vessel of US popular culture and national identity.

Michael Coyne, *Hollywood Goes to Washington* [1]

The use of metaphors such as 'mirror', 'barometer' and 'vessel' to describe the American political film is fairly telling of the close and yet complex connection between this particular 'genre' and its real life referent, i.e. the world of American politics. This intimate bond renders *Wag the Dog* particularly apt for exploring the relation between cinema and reality in yet another way, namely by focusing on its portrait of the world of politics and its outlook on the viewers' potential for changing the reality around them.

So far, I have demonstrated the growing complexities in the film/reality bipolar, indicating a series of formal and modal elements in the film's construction that challenged a number of established narrative and semiological norms in analogue fiction filmmaking. Furthermore, I discussed how this particular film and its afterlife short-circuited the distance that separates the filmic from the afilmic reality, suggesting new ways for conceptualizing the relation between these two different ontological levels. Here, I would like to continue the investigation of this relation by returning to the filmic text in order to examine the conventions of the political film and its implications about the role of individuals in the political process. Films about politics are, by definition, engaged in addressing the personal actions and responsibilities of the characters in a political environment, indicating the ways in which they can, or most often cannot, make a difference in the world. Transforming reality to a better (or worse) cause is what constitutes the core of politics and, thus, thematically speaking *Wag the Dog* is once again ideal for unraveling a rather idiosyncratic side of Hollywood filmmaking.

This chapter will approach the triptych politics–Hollywood–reality in three parts; first, I will dwell on the obstacles involved in solidifying a stable generic identity for films that deal with politics, arguing that the peculiar 'cultural verisimilitude'[2] of these films unsettles the expectations of the industry and the audience alike. Second, I will explore *Wag the Dog*'s depiction of American politics, concentrating on the topic of agency and indicating various types of 'actors' in the political game. In its portrayal of the political scene in the United States in the late 1990s, Levinson's film, I would like to argue, puts forward a considerably different outlook on contemporary politics; it challenges the traditional faith in individual agency and foregrounds the role of contingency and complexity in the contemporary globalized world order. Finally, I will retread the history and theory of the American political movie in search for various approaches to human agency vis-à-vis the political system. Here, I will discuss certain notable cases such as *The Candidate*, *The Parallax View*, *Primary Colors* (1998) and *The Ides of March*. Then, I will contrast those fictional accounts of the political world with a supposedly 'real' one found in the widely acclaimed documentary *The War Room*. Once again, the problem of drawing boundaries in the reel/real world will come to the fore, as the books comes full circle with the discussion of the fiction/non-fiction distinctions.

Defining the 'political film'

> Many movies were thus caught in a tug of war between edification and entertainment, between problem raising and happy endings. Under these conditions, relatively few films turned out to be overtly political.
>
> Andrew Sarris, *Politics and Cinema*[3]

Whether messages should be sent through Western Union or through movies has been widely debated among filmmakers and critics alike. Even though the industry's policy promoted the entertaining side of the films, it has become common knowledge that *all* films, explicitly or not, convey messages and affect public consciousness in ways that have yet to be fully explained. Amidst the bulk of films that are produced in Hollywood, there are those few that openly address significant political, historical or social issues in an effort to raise public awareness and even stir controversy in the audience. In this list, one could include examples as diverse as *Casablanca* (1942), *Cabaret* (1972), *The Godfather* (1972), *Platoon* (1986), *JFK* (1991) and *Primary Colors*. Films like these are often characterized as 'political' for touching upon themes related to ideology, society, race or identity, and for resisting the innocuous formula of a Hollywood happy ending.[4] However, the definition of the 'political' still remains broad enough. If we choose to narrow it down, then we should consider as 'political films' only those that deal with the world of American institutional politics per se, featuring political figures and political processes, such as elections and campaigns. Why would that be necessary? Because a more precise definition of the 'political' and a more 'exclusive' list[5] of political films will enable us to clarify whether the political film can be construed as a concrete genre alongside the musical or the western.

So far, prominent theoreticians of the filmic genres have not designated a separated space for the 'political film' on the generic map of Hollywood cinema. For instance, Steve Neale's thorough account presented in *Genre and Hollywood* briefly mentions some political films, in the strictest sense, under the categories of 'social problem film' and 'drama'.[6] On the other hand, Stephen Prince entitles his essay 'Political Film in the Nineties', but his scope in fact includes what he calls 'socially conscious filmmaking' whose genealogy begins with Griffith's *Intolerance* (1916). The problem of defining the political film has been particularly stressed in those, relatively few, publications that examine the cinema where American politics is in sharp focus. Among those is Michael Coyne's book *Washington Goes to Hollywood* published in 2008. Coyne accounts for the dearth of book-length studies on films about politics by pointing to the fact that the narratives in question have not been accorded the status of a distinct genre. Whereas the western, the musical or even the film noir have been minutely theorized by film academics in myriads of publications, the 'political genre' has evaded such scholarly attention so far. According to Coyne, this significant oversight could be attributed to the fact that the political film[7] amounts to 'a genre by virtue of content than form', while being 'essentially fluid' and 'trans-generic'.[8] All three claims, however, are equally problematic and theoretically obtuse. The 'content versus form' dichotomy has not proved particularly functional within genre theory, whereas other more nuanced approaches, such as Rick Altman's semantic/syntactic approach, have been more successful in delineating the fine boundaries of each genre as well as its transformations.[9] For instance, one could easily identify a series of semantic elements that constitute the core of the political genre, including politicians and institutional processes, as well as a specific iconography that comprises establishing shots of public buildings, close framings of office spaces and even a distinct dressing mode. Moreover, the relations of those semantic elements could easily be framed within various syntaxes, the fluctuations of which could justify the renewal of the genre across time. It is likely that the political film in the 1930s veered towards the structures of melodrama with a more Manichean approach to politics, whereas later on in the 1960s it adopted the syntax of the suspense thriller to emphasize the role of conspiracy in politics at the time. Such could be the reasoning within a semantic/syntactic approach, which also invalidates Coyne's other two characteristics, i.e. fluidity and hubridity. Even though it is commonly felt that all genres change over time and step into each other's territory, the most theoretically astute explanation on these matters is found in Steve Neale's article 'Questions of genre'. There, he argues that genres are better understood as 'processes' dominated by repetition as well as difference, variations and change.[10] Thus, fluidity is not an essential quality of the political film that thwarts definition. In fact, all genres are inherently fluid, urging us to sharpen our tools for capturing their process-like nature. At the same time, Neale notes that hybrids are by no means a rarity in Hollywood as many would have us believe. Quite the contrary; nearly all films could be considered hybrids to the extent that they tend to combine a romance plot with others.[11]

Furthermore, Coyne's lack of a theoretical scaffolding to construct the political genre prevents him from capitalizing on his otherwise insightful observations regarding political films. For instance, in his introduction he embraces Arthur M. Schlesinger Jr.'s framework of 'paradoxes' within American history, such as Experiment/Ideology, Equality/Tolerance of Inequality, Order/Violence, Conformity/Diversity, Materialism/Idealism and America as Redeemer/America as One Nation Among Many. However, the heuristic value of these binary oppositions remains underexploited. Instead of exploring the potential of a structuralist approach to the genre, indicating how these oppositions unearth an underlying structure as well as a stable frame for generating meaning in political films,[12] he is merely content to offer a few scattered film examples that embody those paradoxes in a rather vague manner. As a result, the lack of a conceptual grid to handle the body of the political films and their generic identity leads Coyne to a rather loose use of the term 'genre', leaving the definition of the political film still hanging.

'Why haven't political films been widely recognized as a genre?' is the question that Terry Christensen also poses in the foreword of his book *Reel Politics* and his answer is grounded more on intuition rather than solid knowledge of genre theory. Maybe, he ponders, it is because they 'lack internal consistency' or because they 'look less alike'.¹³ Apart from these casual remarks, however, he adds, somewhat inadvertently, a new critical dimension to this problem when he writes that 'perhaps a part of the reluctance to recognize a political film genre rises from the old fear that Sam Goldwyn spoke of: the fear that the very word "political" will scare moviegoers away'.¹⁴ This observation brings into the frame two other significant parameters of genre constitution, namely the industry and the audience. Genres were traditionally formulas that served the purposes of the classical studios, enabling them to plan production, distribution and exhibition in order to cater for the tastes of a wide audience. Whether it was the industry or the audience that dictated which formulas would find success and would develop into a stable genre is open to debate. The 'ritual approach' argues that the consumers' preferences induce the studios to produce films that reflect their desires, while the 'ideological approach' claims that it is Hollywood which guides those preferences and manipulates them for its own interest.¹⁵ In response to these two opposing frames, Altman uses his semantic/syntactic approach to propose a compromising middle ground:

> The structures of Hollywood cinema, like those of American popular mythology as a whole, serve to mask the very distinction between ritual and ideological functions. Hollywood does not simply lend its voice to the public's desires, nor does it simply manipulate the audience. On the contrary, most genres go through a period of accommodation during which the public's desires are fitted to Hollywood's priorities (and vice-versa).¹⁶

In light of this assertion, the question as to why the 'political genre' never entered the inventory of the classical Hollywood genres, despite the success and the critical recognition of many political films, could be rephrased as follows: why hasn't the political formula evoked a lasting fit between the audience's needs and the industry's objectives? Or, in other words, why both Hollywood and the audience tacitly 'agreed' that the political film could be an occasional luxury but not a steady occurrence in the Hollywood output?

Emblematic of the uneasiness with which Hollywood often handles political films, is the case of Levinson's *Man of the Year*, which was promoted as a comedy about politics. The poster features Robin Williams with a smug face and a wig a là George Washington, while the tagline asks 'Could this Man be Our Next President?' The marketing campaign of the film capitalized on William's comic persona to invite the audience to another hilarious parody of the American political scene. Yet, the film was nothing like that. In fact, the story of the

TV comedian-turned-president openly raised a number of serious political concerns in the era of the internet and digital technology, alarming us about the threats of hyperreality against the core values of democracy. The discrepancy between the marketing of the film and its actual content was immediately noted by the viewers' community in various reviews and blogs.[17] It is worth quoting one IMDB user, in particular, as he seems to touch upon the difficult balance between what the industry proposes and what the audience wants.

> Man anyone walking into this film expecting to see a brainless comedy will surely be disappointed. I always wonder how some people are film marketers when I see how misleading their marketing campaigns. 'Man of the Year' is a great example of bad and misleading marketing, because everything from the poster, to the trailer, to the online advertisements makes this movie look and feel like a comedy. I would honestly have to say about 1/3 of the film is funny while the rest of it plays off as a political thriller that makes good arguments and allows its audience to think. I kind of wonder in this case if the marketing was done on purpose since this film addresses pretty serious issues in-between its comedy routine.[18]

The marketing strategy of *Man of the Year* backfired on the film in the effort to conceal its true narrative premises and to play down its strong political overtones. On the other hand, it is hard to guess whether its box office success would have been greater had the studio revealed its true colors. The lack of a distinct political genre at the institutional level is also coupled by a lack of specific 'systems of expectation and hypothesis' that viewers could use in their interaction with this type of films. This aspect of genre formation is emphasized by Neale when he argues that genres are not simply bodies of films, no matter how they are classified and defined.[19] Genres equally consist of an interpretative framework and a horizon of expectations that are at once stable and varied, repeated or transformed, just as it happens with the generic conventions at the filmic level. My argument is that one of the primary reasons why the political film was not constituted as a genre, neither from the side of Hollywood nor the audience, is the inherent problem of these films with the issue of 'cultural verisimilitude'. In other words, the difficulty that has been repeatedly noted[20] in the creation of a separate branch on the Hollywood tree of genres does not lie in the absence of a textual coherence or the mixture with other generic plots (comedy/thriller), but rather in the inability of the industry and the spectators alike to handle the implications that these films bear on the relation between the cinema and the real world. I believe a number of clarifications are in order.

Every genre entails a different system of expectations and hypotheses that the spectators can rely on for comprehending and interpreting a film that belongs to it. For example, when somebody goes to watch a musical, it is unlikely that they will be startled by the song and dance that will eventually take over the screen. Similarly, in a romantic comedy, they expect to have a fairly happy ending and not the tragic death of the heroine. These expectations are shaped by two broad types of verisimilitude: generic and social or cultural verisimilitude.[21] The generic verisimilitude controls what seems realistic and probable according to the internal rules of each genre. For instance, a horror film will be considered realistic if there is a monster that spreads fear to the characters. On the other hand, the monster tends to be much less realistic in terms of its cultural verisimilitude, as we don't regularly come across monsters in our everyday life. In other words, the generic verisimilitude dictates what we should expect according to the rules of the game in each genre, while the cultural verisimilitude holds the real world as a referent for what might be probable or not. Several genres, such as the musical, melodrama or science fiction have developed a generic verisimilitude that contradicts or at least disregards the norms of cultural verisimilitude. Fewer genres, however, like the war film or the period drama, ground their realism on the use of authentic sources and documents, but they are also generically allowed to exaggerate and magnify their stories for the purposes of spectacle. My contention is that the more a genre appeals to the norms of cultural verisimilitude, the more controversial it tends to become. And as many scholars have noted, successful Hollywood filmmaking thrives on conflict but not on controversy.[22]

Thus, we have reached the core of the problem that tantalizes each political film; its inevitable relation to the real world. Unlike any other genre film, a film about American politics cannot portray a story about politicians and procedures in a way entirely independent of what people perceive them to be in real life. And given that politics bears direct and constant consequences on every American citizen's life, the political subject matter is not easy to single out, process and mythologize without risking controversy. Nor can generic verisimilitude offer a creative refuge to filmmakers for escaping the pressures of reality. It would be hard to imagine a series of intrinsic conventions that could *systematically* allow politicians to behave or elections to occur in entirely unrealistic fashions. Granted, the mixture with comedy or the suspense thriller allows political films to incorporate humorous situations or emotionally intense plot reversals, but the ultimate question that haunts each viewer at the exit of the film theatre is: is that really true?

One could argue that the same question creeps up on us when we watch war films or historical films in general. Indeed, these two genres have also been difficult to accommodate in the regular Hollywood agenda, as the potential for controversy is considerably higher. The reason why war and history did manage to carve a distinct space, however minor, in the Hollywood generic land could be related to issues of temporality and identification. War films portray situations usually located in the historical past where there is a specific conflict and a clearly demarcated enemy that the Americans are fighting against. Before the advent of television, the relation between cinema and war was admittedly more contemporaneous, as the case of World War II testifies. At the time, Hollywood solidified the war genre by producing a number of films before and during the US involvement in order to mobilize the audience. But the audience obviously wanted to be mobilized too. A lasting fit, to remember Altman, was made possible by the fact that the spectators could unite against a common enemy and envision a better world without fascism. Would a similar spread of war films be likely about the war in Afghanistan? The answer is probably no. With television and other media covering the spectators' needs for information about the present and the future, and given the ideological ambivalence of the American public about the US foreign policy, war films in Hollywood can only be safely engaged with the past.

On the other hand, a film about American politics inherently carries questions about the possibilities in the present and the future, even if it deals with a political event or a scandal of the past, as in *All the President's Men* (1976) or *Good Night and Good Luck* (2005). The transcendental issues that accompany each political film, such as the role of democracy, the place of the individual in the political system, the function of power and justice, are difficult to isolate from the specific plot that the film portrays and, thus, always tend to resonate with contemporaneous political concerns. Thus, the inherent qualities of the theme of American politics render it difficult for the industry to produce a regular output of political films for a wide audience. At the same time, the American citizens seem equally reluctant to ponder on questions about their role in democracy on a regular basis. Unlike in war films, the enemy in political stories is located within American society and within each human individual. It would seem unlikely that a large number of spectators would be willing to look at themselves in the mirror every time they entered the movie theatre.

The close ties of the political narratives with their surrounding reality are also evidenced in the frequent exchange of roles between Hollywood and

Washington.²³ Several of the writers and directors of political films are actively involved in politics either as speechwriters, advisers or activists, blurring the distinction between real and reel politics to such a degree that, sometimes, scripts need to be greenlit by senators.²⁴ The case of Jeremy Larner, the writer of *The Candidate* is fairly telling. He started out as a journalist in the early 1960s and entered the political scene in 1968 as a speechwriter for Eugene McCarthy in his campaign for the presidency. Three years later Larner wrote the script of *The Candidate*, which unsettled many senators but won him the Oscar for best original screenplay in 1973. From then on, he would occasionally return to speechwriting for politicians, a solid proof of how fiction and reality are often made of the same material. Similarly, the producer of *Bob Roberts* (1991), Forrest Murray, impressed the Democratic National Committee with the accuracy of his depiction of the campaign mannerisms in the film and he was hired to make a short feature for the California State Democratic Party convention.²⁵ This type of exchange of labour justifies why the level of cultural verisimilitude in political films is regularly so high, while in some cases, like the aforementioned *Bob Roberts* and of course *Wag the Dog*, the sense of 'verisimilitude' takes on the shape of authenticity or even prophesy.²⁶

Overall, the political film has its long idiosyncratic trajectory in the history of American cinema and, despite its controversial nature, it sustains its role as a 'barometer' and 'vessel' of American society, to remember Coyne's aforementioned statement. *Wag the Dog* has so far been an ideal case study for exploring the relation between cinema and reality in the contemporary age, and its generic identity offered us another opportunity in this section to examine this relation from the point of view of genre. Now it is time we delved into the image of the political world that springs out of this film and discuss the representation of US politics in the modern world.

Wag the Dog and US politics

Wag the Dog's portrait of the world of politics is all inclusive; the President, the communication strategists, the public and the media take positions in a crammed frame that accommodates conflicting interests and diverse perceptions of the issues at stake. My goal is to view this picture through the prism of agency, i.e. by asking the seemingly basic question 'who does what', in an effort to identify the competing forces in the contemporary political environment.

Back in Chapter 1, I discussed the matter of narrative agency, examining the levels on which the film's narration is built. The conclusions drawn from the formal analysis regarding the multiplicity of narrative agents, the dubiousness of the narrative techniques and the narrative prominence of objects, such as television screens, are reflected in turn in the content of the film where the matter of agency is handled in a rather ambivalent fashion. Besides, the extradiegetic question 'why does a dog wag its tail' and the subsequent propositions ('because a dog is smarter than its tail' and 'if the tail were smarter, it would wag the dog') pose in an enigmatic, if playful manner, the problem of causation and instrumentality.

At this point, it is useful to keep in mind how classical Hollywood cinema has established a very consistent model of agency, which relies on the action hero as a rational and goal-oriented individual. The classical narratives feature a character-centred causality that places the individual motivation at the centre of the plot, while all other forces, such as chance or natural phenomena, play a background role that probes but does not determine the action.[27] The strong faith in the human initiative was briefly shaken in the late 1960s and early 1970s when a series of young American filmmakers chose to proclaim what Thomas Elsaesser dubbed the 'pathos of failure'.[28] In films like *Easy Rider* (1969), *Bonnie and Clyde* (1967), *Two-lane blacktop* (1971), *Five easy pieces* (1970), *The last detail* (1973) and *California split* (1974) the protagonists lack a clear-cut motivation and fail to embody a determinate goal. According to Elsaesser, the lack of motive in the characters' actions and the loose progression of the plot were indicative of skepticism towards the ideals of American society and the traditional belief in personal initiative.[29] Whereas classical Hollywood maintained a solid faith in human agency, rational judgement and the fulfillment of goals, the sensibility of the New Hollywood, albeit in its brief history, adopted a more pessimistic stance about the possibility to solve all problems, to face all obstacles. But what about the state of American pragmatism in the late 1990s? Does *Wag the Dog* sustain a faith in human resolve or is it no longer in one's hands to change the world? In what follows, I will track the 'actors' in the political arena, dividing them into two categories, namely the human and the non-human actors, to see how the power of influence is distributed in the film and to discuss the implications of this type of distribution for American democracy.

What individuals do (or don't do)

In a film about American politics and, more specifically, about a presidential crisis, the physical absence of the President from the screen makes a powerful statement about his role in the political game that plays out in the plot. Everything revolves around the President, his image and his race for re-election, and yet his actual figure is never to be seen. It does not matter for the viewer who he is, what he looks like or how he thinks, as most decisions are taken by those in charge of his communication strategy. All he has to do is follow their orders religiously. And when the film allows him to intervene, it is only to stress how unimportant or even pitiful he is.

First and foremost, all communication with the President is carried through Ames, who regularly calls him on her cell phone to keep him updated about their plans. A few minutes into the film we watch Brean give orders about the President's return from China, while later he chooses the airport in which his plane will land and even choreographs his entire performance in front of the gathered crowd. Brean's instructions are implemented down to the last detail, causing the President to appear as the ultimate puppet. On the few occasions that the President calls up the team and tries to intervene, he is treated as a distraction or even a nuisance. A parody of his impotence is made during the shooting of the war scene, where we witness a lengthy dispute over the type of kitten that will be digitally inserted into the video. The President is adamant about the use of a white kitten and his wish is disgruntledly respected at the threat of mobilizing the 6th fleet.

The President's lack of agency is also illustrated in Levinson's mise-en-scène in the segment of the speech about Sergeant Schumann. Initially, the President refuses over the phone to give the speech because he finds it corny. Motss is infuriated by his resistance and tries to prove the emotional strength of the speech by reading it in front of 20 secretaries in the White House. We catch a glimpse of the President's back (Figure 4.1), as he watches the secretaries' reactions and experiences the effectiveness of Motss' words. His change of mind is not even discussed in the film; all we need to see is the team's complacency about the speech's resonance. Not even the actual announcement of the speech on television becomes an opportunity to see the President in some kind of action. Instead, the autocue takes over, giving him precise instructions not only about what to say, but also how to say it (Figure 4.2). We hear his voice perform the task with precision but the camera persistently, and quite ostensibly, deprives

# Figure 4.1

# Figure 4.2

# Figure 4.3

us of his face. In Figure 4.3 we see how the narration blocks the view of the President's televised image by keeping it out of focus. This blatant blockage of the President's face is the ultimate proof of how *Wag the Dog* refuses to acknowledge the President of the United States as an active agent in American politics.

Equally absent are all politicians though. The only political figure that appears in the film is Senator Neal, the presidential opponent, but one could hardly consider him as an independent political spirit. First of all, the film's narration allows him to come forth only through three brief news pieces broadcast on television. This constrained framing already compromises his role as a player in the plot, while his televised statements further exhibit him as being towed in the communication scheme about the Albanian War. The confusion about the agency in the film is crystallized in the following dialogue:

> NEAL (on TV): I have just gotten word ... that the situation in Albania is resolved ... that it is resolved. The CIA confirms ... that our troops along the Canadian border ... and overseas are standing down. I must take this opportunity to call upon our president ...
> MOTSS: What does he mean, the situation has been resolved?
> BREAN: He just ended the war.

MOTSS: *He* ended the war?
AMES: Why did he have to go and do that?
BREAN: I think the CIA cut a better deal.
MOTSS: *He* ended the war? He can't end the war. He's not producing this.

In the communication war that the leading protagonists waged against Albania, the various sources of agency vie for prominence without realizing, with the exception of Brean, the contingencies of this new type of power play. Motss is baffled to see somebody else end what he considers to be *his* war but the film clearly points out that, once you enter the communication process, authorship is no longer possible to maintain.

The portrayal of politicians in the film differs greatly from most other representations in the history of American cinema. The American president in the film is partly present and partly absent, a fact that compromises his human qualities whether good or bad. Whenever the American president was absent from the political setting in other films ranging from *Mr Smith Goes to Washington* (1939) to *The Candidate* and later *Bulworth* (1998), it meant that he was allowed 'to remain above the corruption, the pettiness, and the partisanship of American party politics while, consequently, symbolizing continuity and strength in face of the challenges to the political system.'[30] Whenever he was present, he could be either idolized as in *Wilson* (1944), or at least be redeemed for his flaws as in *Primary Colors*. Even critical portrayals of admittedly controversial presidents, like Richard Nixon or George W. Bush, would offer the viewers some entry points into their personalities, helping them empathize to some extent with their weaknesses. Choosing to focus on the President and yet strip him of any human characteristics (even his alleged infidelity is not considered pertinent to the story) indicates an entirely novel approach to human agency that reduces all activity to its communicational value.

In this context, the juxtaposition of the two male characters helps the film strengthen its position about reality and justice as 'special effects', as we discussed in previous chapters. The contrasting personalities of the two protagonists emulate an antithesis between the classically motivated hero that has dominated the entire tradition of Hollywood filmmaking and a new type of hero that we could call the 'performative agent', who is beginning to appear in a number of films in the new millennium.[31] It is more appropriate to begin our analysis with Motss, the classical hero, as his character is more familiar and more accessible to us.

Motss is portrayed as an eccentric and talented Hollywood producer who lives in Los Angeles in a typically luxurious mansion. He has an army of attendants to cater to his whims and he likes giving orders left and right in a loud voice. Among his redeemable features, though, one can note his incredible sense of humor and his child-like enthusiasm that make him popular among the people around him. Motss is fascinated by the challenge to produce a fake war in order to distract public opinion for 11 days and secure the President's re-election. Being in Hollywood all his life, this sounds like the absolute mission, with a tight deadline to keep him focused on his target. The fact that he handles the situation as merely another Hollywood production is evidenced on several occasions. One of his first concerns is to establish a clear plotline about the war with a logical cause-and-effect chain of events. Within minutes he comes up with the perfect pitch: a war against Albania because the United States has just found out that Albanian terrorists have placed a suitcase bomb in Canada in an attempt to infiltrate it into the country and destroy the American way of life. His years of experience in Hollywood narratives helps him churn out a very coherent rationale for this war but when he begins to talk about Act I and II, Brean stops him and explains that there will not be an Act II. Motss immediately resumes his enthusiasm, exclaiming: 'It's a teaser!'

The discussion about the acts of the drama will eventually come back in the second half of the film when the protagonists watch the end of the war on TV in the aforementioned scene. At that moment, Motss' reaction triumphantly confirms his classically defined motivation, as he shouts 'No, the war isn't over till I say it's over. This is *my* picture. This is not CIA's picture' and then promptly adds, 'This is nothing. This is nothing. This is just Act I: The War. Now we really need an Act II.' Being a typical action hero, Motss' morale is only boosted by each difficulty he encounters. His ambition would never allow him to give up his mission and the gratification of a happy ending is summed up in his final comment, worth repeating here: 'This is a complete fucking fraud and it looks 100 per cent real. It's the best work I've ever done in my whole life, because it's so *honest*.'[32]

Wag the Dog's take on politics is not akin to the classical Hollywood tradition though. After the classical hero accomplishes his mission, it is time for the other actors in the game and, principally, Brean to remind the viewer that there is no happy ending to the narrative, and in fact, there is no ending at all, as the final moment suggests.[33] The desire for closure and, thus, for acknowledgement of his masterpiece on the part of Motss is perfectly reasonable from his point of view. The hero accomplishes a mission in order to be rewarded, in order to get the credit. The classical trajectory is thwarted here because the organizational scheme of the film only partly works as a classical narrative. The other dynamics are best embodied in Brean's personality who introduces a new logic into the action.

Brean enters the diegesis, as we saw in Chapter 1, from multiple levels of narration, a fact that amplifies his narrative significance. We hear from Ames that he is 'Mr Fix-it' but, apart from this comment, his professional identity is never fully spelled out. In fact, the film emphasizes the ambiguity surrounding his line of work by having Motss ask him on three separate occasions 'exactly what do you do for the President' and not getting any answer. The dominant trait of this character is his distant procedural attitude towards the problem in hand. Whereas Motss is genuinely enthusiastic and engrossed in the mission, Brean maintains a level of calmness and aloofness throughout the film. He, too, is interested in results and he oversees closely the progression of the enterprise but, at the same time, he remains emotionally detached from it.

The difference of involvement between Motss and Brean, I believe, is rooted in a discrepancy in the perception of the task in question. Motss is a true believer; he takes up the staging of the Albanian war and sees it through the end, as if it were a real thing. Hence the 'honesty' he mentioned above or his frequent confusion between reality and fiction, as when he seriously suggests the President should win a peace prize. Brean, on the other hand, considers the entire scheme as a performance based solely on the handling of information, regardless of its relation to an external reality. As we discussed in Chapter 2, one of his credos is that there cannot be a clear distinction between fact and fiction and, therefore, he takes every sign or every image for what it *does* and not what it *is*. This is why, unlike the rest of the team, he is not surprised or angry when other actors in the game, like the CIA or Senator Neal, change the flow of information. His emphasis on performance is most compelling in his conversation with Mr Young, the CIA officer who confronts him with evidence of the absence of the war. While Ames is shaking like a leaf trying to come up with silly excuses, Brean sits back confidently and waits for his turn to present a fully-blown rationale for the war. His final statements are worth quoting at length:

> And if you go to war again, who is it going to be against? Your ability to fight a Two-ocean War against who? Sweden and Togo? Who you sitting here to Go To War Against? That time has passed. It's passed. It's over. The war of the future

is nuclear terrorism. It is and it will be against a small group of dissidents who, unbeknownst, perhaps, to their own governments, have blah blah blah. And to go to that war, you've got to be prepared. You have to be alert, and the public has to be alert. Cause that is the war of the future, and if you're not gearing up, to fight that war, eventually the axe will fall. And you're gonna be out in the street. And you can call this a drill, or you can call it job security, or you can call it anything you like. But I got one for you: you said, Go to war to protect your Way of Life, well, Chuck, this is your way of life. Isn't it? And if there ain't no war, then you, my friend, can go home and prematurely take up golf. Because there ain't no war but ours.

His little speech about the war of the future sounds overwhelming or even plausible simply because it resonates with some of the standard notions of American exceptionalism, such as the supremacy of the American way of life or the role of America as a redeemer nation. His skilful rhetoric and clever sophistry are his most powerful weapons in a power game that is mostly dependent upon appearances. No wonder why Ames exclaims enthusiastically afterwards that he gave a 'phenomenal performance'.

What is intriguing about *Wag the Dog* is how it takes an utterly outrageous premise, a fake war against a small European country very far from the United States, and yet, underneath the surface, it creates a rather nuanced portrait of American politics. With Motss being 100 per cent immersed in the fiction of the war, and with Ames making constant reality checks, Brean succeeds in carving a separate path where neither fiction nor reality is pertinent. This is why he hardly thinks of his job in terms of 'lying' or 'manipulating' or 'making a conspiracy', as one would probably expect. This is also why after the meeting with the CIA, we only hear him say 'they just hadn't thought it through' instead of bragging about 'tricking' or deceiving them. According to Brean, politics is communication and communication is a complex and fluid process that entails certain variables, such as human and non-human agents, while it depends on measurable as well as contingent parameters such as deadlines, speed and chance. In this process, he cannot help but admit that he is only an agent among many whose only choice is to adapt his own performance according to the communication flow. In this light, the fact that he orders Motss' death without a second thought and then shows up at his funeral comes across as another act emptied of any moral or emotional significance. It is simply his share in the ongoing performance.

What objects do

In addition to the protagonists, objects also perform in *Wag the Dog*. As the narrative analysis has disclosed already, objects are planned to play a prominent role in the story. It is particularly the presence of television that claims an equal diegetic function with the human characters in the plot. As I have argued, this function instigates impersonal levels of narration, while it also enhances the realistic motivation in the film, which thrives on the notion of immediacy and speed.[34] From the political point of view though, the use of TV sets in the *Wag the Dog* is equally significant. Their omnipresence testifies a new level of interference with the human activities, probing us to reconsider some of our traditional notions of causality.

Classical heroes would always accomplish their missions with some kind of aid from objects but those objects would hardly be considered as sources of agency. The classical Hollywood narration would make sure that the character-centred action and the continuity system would not allow the viewers to lift their eyes from the magnitude of the individual. This is hardly the case, though, in *Wag the Dog*. From start to finish, the film promulgates the importance of media in modern politics, elevating a significant weight of responsibility from the human shoulders. Even though specific individuals like journalists, publicists and politicians work with the media to generate ideas and materials, the outstanding prominence of technology and media messages in the film attributes the latter with a life of their own. Apart from the opening (the presidential TV spot) and the closure (a news bulletin), the entire story world is inhabited visually and aurally by media artefacts. In some cases they are collaborators in the grand scheme, while in others they change the protagonists' plans and force them to adapt to new conditions. In other words, human and non-human agents in the film contribute equally to the progression of the story and, thus, could be held equally accountable for the problematic state of American politics in the contemporary age. The scene with the live press conference at the White House, highlighted for the element of immediacy in Chapter 2, is also emblematic of the human/non-human agency. Motss' large TV screen, Ames' cell-phone and the spokesman's earphone, so clearly demonstrated by the latter's gesture (Figure 4.4), are not mere channels but equal participants in the ongoing communication process, whose aim is to establish the measure of intervention in the political events.

Figure 4.4

Before elaborating further on the implications of this new type of human/non-human agency, there is another plot element worth discussing in some detail regarding its ideological underpinnings. Throughout the film we see a growing competition between the President's official publicity campaign and the hidden enterprise speared by Brean. In a way, we witness a conflict between old style public relations and a new communication strategy with different conceptual stakes. When Motss watches the TV spot with the horses and listens to the 'Don't change horses in mid-stream' slogan, he bursts out yelling 'Why are they sticking with this age old horseshit? Why are they sticking with the same garbage? Who hires these people?!' In fact, it is his indignation with the traditional PR talk he hears on a TV show that causes him to lose his life. The journalists and the political analysts ponder on the tremendous change in the President's popularity after the Albanian crisis, trying to enlighten the voters about the role of 'spinning' the events, the impact of commercials and the packaging of the President as a 'product'. Motss' reaction is only too justified. The entire film we have just watched has plainly demonstrated that the effectiveness of traditional PR strategies is a thing of the past. The process of media manipulation has been taken to the next level where spinning the events is no longer sufficient; the events now have to be fabricated altogether to serve the political purposes of the President or any other powerful figure. When approaching these two distinct communication 'strategies' one is confronted with a different set of underlying assumptions. The traditional public relations could be easily deconstructed by unveiling the publicity techniques, the selling tricks and the elements of the 'spectacle', while maintaining a strong footing on the humanist and idealist values, such as truth and justice. In other words, the manipulation could be pinpointed, analysed and even neutralized, if one had the necessary insight and will. In the new state of things, this road cannot be taken. The external 'reality' and the veracity of facts are out of reach. In fact, they are not even pertinent. What seems to be pertinent though is to watch closely the performance and do what Bruno Latour suggests, to 'follow the actor'.[35]

And this brings me to the theoretical template of political action that, I believe, *Wag the Dog* puts forward. It is a template that breaks away from the traditional subject-centred perspectives and introduces two key system-centred premises; i) the equal distribution of agency among human and non-human actors, according to Latour's Actor-Network Theory, and ii) the approach of the political system as an 'autopoetic system', according to Niklas Luhmann's line of thought. First, Latour in *Reassembling the Social* (2005) offers a concise introduction to the so-called Actor-Network Theory, a theoretical framework formulated by himself and other social thinkers like John Law and Michel Callon, who aimed to redefine our notion of the 'social' by reinstating, among other things, the role of objects in human societies.[36] Latour explains how the source of action cannot be located in human entities only and, in fact, it cannot be located in a single point at all. Instead, action can be conceived only as the result of a network of actors, both human and no-nhuman, associated momentarily to modify a state of affairs.[37] As my preceding analysis has shown, *Wag the Dog*'s narrative both in terms of style and in its plot development emulates the principles of actor-network theory in a fashion that, just like the theory itself, cannot but leave us puzzled. Humans as we are, it is uncustomary for us to realize the agency of things and to understand the hybridity of existence in all its dimensions, particularly since such concession would force us to reconsider the powers of rational and will-bound individuality.[38]

And our position becomes even more compromised within Luhmann's systemic approach to media and other institutions. Brean's treatment of media communication and his emphasis on performance seem as if Levinson, Mamet and the other creative collaborators in the film had listened carefully to Luhmann's lectures about the reality of mass media.[39] Brean's views on the function of television and its construction of reality echo Luhmann's approach to mass media as closed autopoetic systems whose one and only purpose is their own self-preservation. Television messages are not regulated by a true/false code but rather by the information/non-information code. This is why Brean does not care whether anything is true or not. All he tries to control is the information that gets transmitted through the media. When he talks about the Gulf War and the smart bomb footage that circulated on the TV screens across the globe, he cannot but shrewdly note 'how the fuck do we know if it was true?'[40] And this is nothing but a slang version of what Luhmann argues below:

> Within the terms of a classical discourse of truth as well as of ordinary, everyday understandings of truth, it would be interesting at this point to know whether that which the media report is true or not true; or if it is half true and half not true because it is being 'manipulated'. But how are we to tell? This may be possible in isolated cases for one or another observer and in particular for the systems being reported on; but for the mass daily flow of communications it is, of course, impossible.[41]

The repercussions of this acknowledgement on the part of social theory are tremendous and, therefore, highly controversial.[42] If we negotiate some of the long-standing presuppositions about an ontological, available, objectively accessible reality, on the one hand, and if we exchange individual will with impersonal communication processes, on the other, then we are left with hardly any vision of a 'better world'. When we could still talk about conspiracies or corruption and when we could still confer moral judgements upon human behaviour, we presumed that the secrets could be disclosed, the mistakes could be corrected and that people were capable of making changes in the world around them. *Wag the Dog* denies this possibility. When the curtain on the Albanian crisis falls and the protagonists leave the (story) world, the TV goes on just the same. The two final shots of the news bulletin and the conference room in the basement of the White House confirm that both the system of mass media and the political system are fully in place; their internal processes are working non-stop for their autopoesis.

US politics in Hollywood

The image of American politics on the screen has been documented in the relatively few books that have embraced an exclusive definition of political films, particularly from the late 1980s onwards.[43] The lack of a clear formal outline of those movies, however, is coupled, as expected, by a lack of a systematic theorization of their ideological underpinnings. The only publication that attempts to formulate a broader schema of the ideological trajectory of the political genre is Coyne's aforementioned *Washington Goes to Hollywood*. According to Coyne, we can identify six discreet phases in the life of the American political film: 1) the mythic/ idealistic; 2) the pragmatic; 3) the paranoiac; 4) the nostalgic;

5) the schizophrenic; and, finally, 6) the apocalyptic.[44] Despite succumbing to the general tendency to cling rather too closely to the linear chronology of the films, Coyne seeks to determine a common dominant ideological current in the films of each distinct period in American history. The 'mythic and idealistic' phase spans three decades, from the 1930 to the 1950s, and it is best exemplified in films such as *Gabriel over the White House* (1930) and *Mr Smith Goes to Washington*. The dominant ideological position of these narratives is to propagate faith in freedom and democracy and to reassert trust in the power of the individual to stand above corruption. The 'pragmatic' phase is significantly briefer; it only includes the first half of the 1960s when John F. Kennedy's presidency managed temporarily to transfuse some hope and optimism for American politics. In films like *Advise and Consent* (1962) and *The Best Man* (1964) the moral message is that good and honest politicians exist and they simply need to prevail in order to serve the American ideals. The second half of the 1960s though, due to the disillusionment surrounding Kennedy and Martin Luther King's assassination, prefigured the third phase, the paranoiac. Even though Coyne signals the beginning of paranoia with John Frankenheimer's trilogy *The Manchurian Candidate* (1962), *Seven Days in May* (1964) and *Seconds* (1966), he claims that the phase took shape in the 1970s when the Vietnam war, the Nixon administration and the Watergate scandal altered for good the American political scene. Apart from *All the President's Men*, which dealt directly with Watergate and in which determined individuals managed to score a victory over political corruption, most other narratives seem to abandon all hope for a better world. Politicians were not merely corrupt; it was the entire power structure that was set to serve the interests of the few against the majority of the American people. Thrillers such as *Executive Action* (1973) and *The Parallax View* portrayed the system as 'imperious, impenetrable and invincible',[45] leaving no possibility for political change. The pessimism of the 1970s gave way with Ronald Reagan's ascent to power in the 1980s, inaugurating the fourth phase, the 'nostalgic'. This phase, as Coyne argues, comprises three diverse Presidents: Reagan, George Bush and the first term of Bill Clinton. During the Reagan years, the narratives concerned with American politics per se came mainly from TV productions, either in the form of mini-series of low profile TV films, which revisited the past glories of Abraham Lincoln or George Washington. Institutional politics returned to the big screen in the early 1990s with *JFK* (1991) and *In the Line of Fire* (1993) looking back at the Kennedy assassination, while Clinton's presence in the Oval Office, initially at

least, spawned romantic comedies like *Dave* (1993) and *The American President* (1995). The nostalgic phase came to an abrupt end in the mid-1990s, when the Oklahoma City bombings and Clinton's misconduct gave the Americans reasons to be wary again of the political system. Coyne characterizes the years 1995–2000 as a 'schizophrenic' phase, when critical films such as *Wag the Dog* and *Bulworth* were coupled with heroic portraits of the president, as in *Independence Day* (1996) and *Air Force One* (1997). Finally, the 9/11 bombings and the USA Patriot Act of 2001 launched an 'apocalyptic' phase in American political cinema, which gave rise to productions such as *The Assassination of Richard Nixon* (2004) and *Good Night and Good Luck* (2005) and inspired the remakes of two classics; *The Manchurian Candidate* (2004) and *All the Kings Men* (2006).

Coyne's schema above is constructive, in the first instance, as it provides a coherent framework for organizing the sum of political films made from the advent of sound cinema until approximately 2008. However, his choice of terms and the lack of a consistent set of criteria for designating each distinct phase results in a rather uneven and often inconsistent categorization of the films in question. For instance, the mythic/idealistic phase lasts for three decades grouping together a number of diverse films, while the more recent phases change almost every five years. Moreover, in what sense is the period 1995–2000 'schizophrenic' other than the fact that the Hollywood output does not form an easily discernible pattern? The task in hand, i.e. the formation of a large-scale model for political films across time, is invaluable but its interpretative value is easily jeopardized unless it adheres to a set of clearly defined and conceptually refined principles. Even though such an enterprise exceeds the purposes of this chapter, I would like to venture a critical reconsideration of a number of political films to see how the concept of 'agency' that I deployed in my reading of *Wag the Dog* could prove useful in detecting various continuities in the body of political films. Instead of using linear chronology and signal historical events to create in a top-down manner a model for the political image of America, I would like to start off with the details; how people and objects act and how are they considered to affect the (political) reality around them. I would like to compare individual agency and will in *The Candidate* and *The Parallax View* from the 1970s and then contrast *Primary Colors* with *The Ides of March* to see how liberal views handle political ethics. Finally, a juxtaposition of those fictional accounts with *The War Room* will examine how the documentary tradition, despite its closer ties with the external reality, treads a similar path with fiction filmmaking when it comes to portraying human behaviour and the forces of causality in the political world.

The Candidate

Michael Ritchie's film starring Robert Redford as a democratic candidate for the US Senate is one of the most widely acclaimed films about politics.[46] Redford plays Bill McKay, a young idealist lawyer, who is convinced to run against Crocker Jarmon, the popular Republican Senator, in order to ... lose. As Andrew Sarris has noted, McKay's motivation for entering such race is not fully justified nor is there any mention of how he would fund his candidacy.[47] In the course of the campaign, McKay succumbs to the rules of the game and adapts to the exigencies of the electoral process. When he unexpectedly wins the election, he cannot but be baffled and wonder 'what do we do now?'

According to Coyne's taxonomy, *The Candidate* was made during the paranoiac phase, when the formidable powers of the 'system' were considered capable of crushing any individual initiative. In a way, the closure of Ritchie's film partly seems to vindicate or, at least, relate to such premise but, before that, we do spend a considerable amount of screen time focusing on Bill McKay as a human in flesh and blood guided by political views, passions and, ultimately, personal decisions. In the beginning, he is an activist who struggles, quite successfully, to defend the rights of the poor and the underprivileged. He holds liberal views that he gets to propagate through his campaign, as he shakes hands with people on the beach or in the black neighborhood. According to the polls, he is not doing badly; he is just winning the votes of the people who already agree with him. The next step would be to try to win over those who don't. To that end, he plays by the rules of the media industry, which seeks to mellow down the message of McKay's politics and sell him as a pretty package with the slogan 'Bill McKay: the better way'. But even then, he risks taking the path of his own individuality; during the live debate with Jarmon on TV, he dares point out that their discussion barely touched upon the key issues of poverty and race. The film rushes to cover up the ramifications of this choice by immediately bringing in the endorsement of McKay's father, which seals the final victory of the Democratic candidate.

Against most liberal readings of this film, which focus on corrupt politics and the hegemony of the system,[48] I would like to argue that *The Candidate* is still a very person-centred narrative that revolves around the decisions and the dilemmas of an admittedly flawed individual. No matter how the media may intervene in the electoral process, McKay can be still held accountable for his role in it. Besides, the combat between McKay and Jarmon is grounded significantly more in real issues rather than media manipulation. Despite the film's attempt to caricature Jarmon's republican politics, he has indeed a very lucid political view summed up as follows: people are responsible for themselves and thus no welfare can change the world, only work can do that. Conservative as that may sound to a liberal viewer, it is a solid position on human behaviour that is not unrelated to the dominant notions of American pragmatism and faith in free will. McKay's position, on the other hand, is less than clear. Otherwise, he would be thrilled to win, despite any compromise he might have made in the process.

The Candidate's take on the media emphasizes the role of the image in American politics, indicating how McKay's good looks and a little help from the TV commercials can alter the candidate's appeal to the public. This is precisely the type of public relations strategies that *Wag the Dog* mocks for their simplicity and naiveté. For the protagonists in Levinson's film selling a politician as a pretty package might have been sufficient in the 1970s but it no longer is in the 1990s, as the media system has acquired new dimensions. The difference of phase between *The Candidate* and *Wag the Dog* is also palpable at the level of style. Ritchie adopts in an open and consistent manner the documentary aesthetics of immediacy that stems from the use of handheld camera, zooming and choppy editing to accentuate the political realism of his story. By exchanging the classical realist mise-en-scène and continuity editing of classical narratives with the documentary techniques of cinema vérité, Ritchie seeks to elevate the cultural verisimilitude of the political tale, which is so key for the entire political genre, as I argued in the opening of this chapter. The same techniques are used only sparingly by Levinson though, adding a rather unsettling effect to the narrating process. *Wag the Dog* does not emulate the form of documentary throughout, but only as a momentary aberration that draws our attention to the narrative agencies at play in the film.

Overall, *The Candidate* depicts the story of a would-be politician who feels appalled by traditional politics and seeks his own trail in the campaigning process. The poster of the film featuring Redford with his mouth covered is, in fact, highly misleading, if not outright inaccurate. The problem with Bill McKay is not that he cannot speak his mind but rather that he cannot make up his mind about what he wants to speak about. As a narrative hero, Bill McKay lacks clear goal-orientation and, therefore, allows other forces, such as his advisors or the media, to intervene and sweep him through. The inability to handle his victory and the powerlessness in front of the prospect of governing the State (i.e. acting), after all, stems more from his personal ineptness rather than the ruthless and invincibly corrupt political system.

The Parallax View

Alan Pakula's *The Parallax View* is one the most notable conspiracy thrillers made during the paranoiac phase of the 1970s. Yet, this time paranoia gets into full swing. The central hero is Joe Frady (Warren Beauty), a newspaper reporter who witnesses the assassination of presidential candidate Senator Charles Carroll atop the Seattle Space Needle on Independence Day. Three years later, seven of the journalists who had been close to the tragedy have been found dead by natural causes. Frady decides to look into one of these deaths and realizes his life is also in danger. One of his findings concerns the obscure workings of an enterprise called The Parallax Corporation, which specializes in 'human engineering'. Frady applies to Parallax under a false name and is successfully recruited as potential criminal material that could be supplied to anyone who pays for it. In his attempt to unveil Parallax's secret operations and, specifically the murder of yet another Senator called George Hammond, Frady is trapped and executed by a Parallax agent. The committee in charge of investigating Hammond's assassination considers Frady as the only perpetrator and, just as in Senator Carroll case, they reject any speculation of a conspiracy theory.

In this political narrative, Frady's character is initially handled in a typically classical Hollywood manner.[49] He is a protagonist defined by a number of recurring motifs, such as his unconventional reporting methods and a knack for women and alcohol. His newspaper editor, Edgar Rintels, urges him to 'curb his talent for creative irresponsibility' but it is precisely this personality flaw that compels Frady to take on such an ambitious and dangerous mission. When Rintels wonders whether they should inform the FBI or the CIA about the role of Parallax in the killings, Frady is convinced that they cannot do anything about it; it is only up to him to reveal the mystery behind this corporation. Thus far, the plot is constructed upon the resolve of the action hero to accomplish his mission and beat the evil forces in the political world. Unlike Bill McKay,

Frady knows exactly what he wants and is not discouraged by the obstacles he encounters. He is determined to go all the way in spite of everybody else's warnings.

Nevertheless, the narrative derails from the classical path as it presents invisible powers stronger than the individual to be in charge of the plotlines. This is what Terry Christensen calls 'the death of a hero'.[50] We witness Frady's efforts to deter Parallax's terrorist actions, but the film openly shows us that the villains are always one step ahead. One notable example is the 'rescue' of the Senator on the plane where a Parallax agent had placed a bomb. The film closely monitors Frady's anxious attempt to warn the crew and ensure the plane's safe return to LA airport. But then, the narration subtly switches levels to show us that the hero is not the subject of the action but rather the object; the bomb incident was merely a test that Parallax had put him through in order to confirm his double agency. In a similar fashion, the final act is initially staged from the protagonist's point of view, as we see him watch the rehearsal of Senator Hammond's political rally. When Hammond is shot down, the film once again reverses Frady's role; from the subject of the gaze he becomes the object of everybody else's searching glare, leading to his death. The hero, thus, is no longer an agent in any sense. Apart from failing to accomplish his mission, Frady also abandons us as a narrative source. The long zooming-out shot on the committee in charge of the inquiry into Hammond's assassination stems from an inconclusive non-diegetic level.

The style and the narration of *The Parallax View* are enormously conducive of the story's key premise, namely that individuals are not in control of their fate. The long geometrical shots of buildings overpowering the human figure, the distant, nearly aseptic, framing of the action and long silent sequences collaborate into a heightened sense of 'impossibility'. The hero cannot act. But then who does? The answer remains deliberately vague. Even though we have a name, Parallax Corporation, and we get to see a few of its representatives, the film refuses to specify the workings of this company and address any economic or political interests that it may serve. Nor does it explain why the specific politicians were targeted. Apart from Senator Carroll's statement about being 'independent', the characters never discuss political matters or opposing ideologies. Both the perpetrators and the victims' motivations remain opaque. In this sense, compared to *The Candidate*'s 'politics corrupts' message and *Wag the Dog*'s 'information feeds the system' credo, *The Parallax View* opts for an even more impersonal, almost metaphysical, approach to evil in human society.

Primary Colors

With *Primary Colors*, we are well into the 1990s and back to a faith in human integrity and ethics. In a way, Coyne is right to call the years 1995–2000 'schizophrenic', especially if we take into account the history of the genre and the dark paths it has trodden through the decades. Mike Nichols' film with John Travolta as Governor Jack Stanton and Emma Thompson as Susan Stanton depicts the workings of a presidential campaign loosely based on Bill Clinton's first run for the presidency in 1992. Indeed, the cultural verisimilitude in this case is exceptionally high on several counts. First, the film is an adaptation of Joe Klein's book of the same name published in 1996, which makes little effort to conceal the connections to real persons and events. Second, Travolta's casting and his overall performance also openly evoke the affinities between Stanton and Clinton's personalities.[51] Finally, the film's release shortly after the Monica Lewinsky scandal amplified the discussions between the reel/real binary that are common in political films, with *Wag the Dog* as the epitome of the implosion of the binary.

Yet, the hero of the film is not Jack Stanton. Despite Travolta's overwhelming personality, the key narrative agent and the central protagonist of the film is Henry Burton (Adrian Lester), the grandson of a respected civil rights pioneer who is invited to join Stanton's stuff as his deputy campaign manager. The entire narrative is presented to us through his point of view, as we see him struggle with his ideals and personal visions. Early on in the film, we have his confession of motivation, which sums up the entire rationale of the story:

> HENRY BURTON: I was always curious about how it would be to work with someone who actually cared about ... I mean ... It couldn't always have been the way it is now. It must have been different when my grandfather was alive. You were there. You had Kennedy. I didn't. I've never heard a president use words like 'destiny' and 'sacrifice' without thinking, 'bullshit'. Okay, maybe it was bullshit with Kennedy, too but ... but people believed it. And, I guess, that's what I want. I want to believe it. I want to be a part of something that's history.

Burton embodies the existential need of the hero to believe in a greater cause and also to regain faith in himself; the hero must stand back on his feet. *Primary Colors* is a neo-romantic tale of individualism that acknowledges the history of American politics and the disillusionment that comes with it but refuses to relinquish the power of the individual to make a difference in the world, to 'make history', as characters often say. Burton enters the political game in a state of demystification and with an avowed need to believe in Stanton's ability to make a difference. But what is it about Stanton that touches him so deeply? The portrait of Stanton as the aspiring president in *Primary Colors* is controversial, but his major strength is pure and simple: he is only human.

Jack Stanton is a warm and sensitive man who lends a sympathetic ear to the underprivileged, ranging from the illiterate to the unemployed. He appears to be emotionally affected by their plight and his tears are not merely an act. He truly empathizes with them and his concern comes across as sincere and unconditional. At the same time, he is characterized by a series of less than appealing traits, such as an insatiable appetite for food and women and a childlike irresponsibility towards punctuality. All these do not trouble Burton; in fact they are considered as part of Stanton's charm. One of the concessions that *Primary Colors* seems to make, vis-à-vis the portrait of the president, is that sleekness and good manners have not done the country much good, so it might be time to bet our money on somebody who is less than perfect but means well.

The problem with acknowledging the human flaws and accepting the grey ethical boundaries in politics comes to the surface when one has to draw a line between compromise and moral defeat. In that regard, *Primary Colors* seeks to test the moral limits of its characters, providing an entry point for almost all possible speaking positions. When Stanton and his wife were presented with the dilemma to disclose or not the dirty secret of their opponent, i.e. Governor Picker's sex and drug issues, 'they didn't even fucking hesitate', to use Libby Holden's (Kathy Bates) exact phrasing. Libby, on the other hand, who had been a close friend of the couple since college and had supported their campaign throughout the film, makes the exact opposite decision and kills herself. The Stanton's lack of moral barriers signified the end of hope and, thus, the end of life for her. The question then turns to Burton and his stance in the debacle. After dithering about it for a while and exchanging views with Stanton about 'the price you pay to lead', the hero chooses to be on the winner's side. Ending on a high note, *Primary Colors* shows us the president's inaugural dance where we see everyone from his staff congratulate him dearly, including Burton. With tears in his eyes, the latter utters the words 'Mr President' and the camera tilts up to show us the American flag.

With this type of closure, Nichols' film offers a counterweight to Levinson's bleak vision of America in the late 1990s. Against *Wag the Dog*'s anti-teleological, systemic approach to politics, *Primary Colors* puts the focus back on the human resources in the making of history. It is neither technology nor the media that set the agenda. Politicians are compelled to factor in the significance of their performance in the media, but it is their personal decisions and their wholehearted struggle that can make a difference in the real world. Commitment and good intentions rank higher than the compromises in politics, as the political ideology of the heroes succumbs to the 'end justifies the means' logic. But would the 'end' of Stanton's political action be so redeeming after all? Taking Clinton's career as a real life answer to that question is not as encouraging.

The Ides of March

One could argue that the knowledge of Clinton's political trajectory as well as other paramount historical events, such as the 9/11 attacks and the war in Iraq, crystallized in the portrait of the politician in George Clooney's *The Ides of March*. In terms of plot development, there are a number of telling similarities with *Primary Colors*, as we once again follow the personal drama of a deputy campaign manager called Stephen Meyers (Ryan Gosling) whose faith in his boss, the Democratic candidate Mike Morris (George Clooney), is challenged when it turns out that Morris is merely another philandering and crooked politician. As in *Primary Colors*, the central hero of the narrative is not the politician but rather his employee. Despite Clooney's star persona attracting most of the publicity, the story concentrates on Meyers' trials and tribulations. Whether this film should be considered as part of the 'apocalyptic' phase of political cinema, according to Coyne's schema, is open to debate, as it would be too soon to decide on such recent productions. What is unequivocal, though, is the fact that the American cinema is still fairly preoccupied with moral boundaries and grey ethical areas in the political life.

All the key characters in *The Ides of March* are distinctively more complex than in previous depictions of the political world. Meyers starts out as a young idealist, just like McKay and Burton before him, claiming that Morris is 'the one' only to be lectured by a *New York Times* reporter that there is no chosen one in this profession; it is only a matter of time before Morris lets him down. With this kind of foreshadowing, and with the aid of Phedon Papamichail's dark cinematography,[52] highly reminiscent of Gordon Willis' work in *The Parallax View*, the film prepares us for a grim development in the plot, which begins as Meyers receives a call from Tom Duffy (Paul Giamatti), the campaign manager of the political opponent. From then on, the motivations and actions of all individuals become increasingly fuzzy. Through a parade of excuses, secrets and revelations, Meyers loses his soul and the human qualities of faith, integrity and loyalty that he so cherished in the beginning. However, the film spends very little screen time pondering on his hurt feelings or his delusion. Unlike Bill McKay, who felt baffled and powerless in the end, and unlike Henry Burton, who resumed his hope in President Stanton as soon as the latter entered the White House, Meyers is transformed into a lifeless automaton; he knows exactly what to say to everyone and how to get what he wants without flinching. The only question left lingering is: to what end is ultimately all that?

In a way, the same question applies to Mike Morris himself. Morris is much too jaded about American politics to think that he could change the country. In a private conversation on the plane early on, Morris is ironic of Meyers' comments about 'doing good to the world' or 'believing in a cause'. Instead of promising to 'make history', he seems to have a very programmatic view of his political career which is summed up merely as 'eight years in the White House'. On the other hand, however, Morris is not portrayed as a pawn in the electoral process. He has a strong opinionated personality, which is not easily manoeuvred by his strategists. Particularly when it comes to the highest stake, the endorsement of Senator Franklin Thomson in exchange of the post of the Secretary of State, Morris is adamant about his uncompromising position until the last closing seconds. As he confesses to his wife: 'Every time I draw a line in the sand ... and I keep moving it. Fundraising, union deals ... I wasn't going to do any of it ... negative ads ... I can't on this one. Not Thompson.' Ironically enough, what moved the line further to include even Thompson was the fear of disclosure of his affair with an intern. Once again, the close ties of the political genre with the real political world are revealed in Meyers' enraged rendition of the following lines: 'Because you broke the only rule in politics. You want to be President, you can start a war, you can lie, you can cheat, you can bankrupt the country, but you can't fuck the interns ... they'll get you for that.' Bill Clinton's painful lesson and the memory of his public humiliation during the Lewinsky scandal seem to have formed a new barrier for the American politician, to which Morris cannot but succumb.

Overall, *The Ides of March*, like many of its predecessors, presents a political tale focused on human decisions and moral choices in the tough world of politics. It is a narrative openly self-conscious about its cinematic pedigree as well as its knowledge of the history of US politics.[53] What is unclear, however, is the subject positioning[54] of the film in the year 2011 in the middle of a world financial crisis and with Barack Obama as the first black American president in the White House. Put differently, one can easily identify the connections of this film with its historic/cinematic past but its resonance with the present and future of American politics is ambiguous. Are we to perceive the human individual as an inherently flawed, albeit powerful, creature that uses political authority for self-serving purposes? And what would these purposes be? Money and power? Ryan Gosling's blank stare at the camera in the closing shot of the film does not provide any conclusive answer to these questions.

The War Room

I would like to conclude this section with an analysis of *The War Room*, a celebrated documentary that promises to reveal the 'real' world of political campaigning. Evidently, this particular comparison between the fictional and the non-fictional depictions of the campaign process is most apt for wrapping up, at this point, the long and multifaceted discussion about the relation between cinema and reality. Already from the taglines used to promote the film on the VHS and DVD covers, one is easily confounded. A quote from *People* magazine calls it 'a remarkably entertaining film', while Janet Maslin's comment from the *New York Times* focuses on the 'cliff-hanging suspense' of the story. Apparently, the institutional barriers that are expected to withhold the collapse of the *textual* barriers between fiction and non-fiction filmmaking, as I argued in Chapter 1, have become even more weakened and untrustworthy.

The viewing expectations triggered by the promotional material of the film are vindicated by the way the renowned filmmaker D. A. Pennebaker and his wife Chris Hegedus chose to present us the real electoral campaign of Bill Clinton, the governor of Arkansas at the time. Their carefully crafted narrative revolves around Clinton's two chief campaign strategists, James Carville and George Stephanopoulos, and their activities between the New Hampshire Primary and the presidential election in 1992. Despite the cinema vérité style of the film, the documentary features an impressively classical plot construction comprising a tight cause-and-effect logic, pressing deadlines, reversals, climactic moments and, above all, a happy ending. Carville and Stephanopoulos are not merely the heroes of *The War Room* but, as the title already suggests, they are attributed all the qualities of the Hollywood war heroes, such as courage, skills and perseverance, that allow them to endure the tough political battles and, finally, prevail over the enemy.⁵⁵ At the same time, both Carville and Stephanopoulos have their weak moments, moments of fear and self-doubt. Their vulnerable and sensitive side makes them even more human in the eyes of the spectator, facilitating further the identification with these characters and their objectives.

But how much of this is real? Or, rather, how much of that story is the real Clinton campaign? What the documentary fails to acknowledge is that the filmmakers shot only 35 hours of footage in a campaign that ran from July to November 1992. In other words, they were allowed to shoot less than 2 days of an activity that lasted four months, while Carville and Stephanopoulos were in total control of what was filmable or not.⁵⁶ In this light, the portrayal of the campaign process and the corollary assumption that Clinton won thanks to the communication strategies presented on screen needs serious reconsideration. It would not be far-fetched to imagine Carville and Stephanopoulos or whoever else was really behind Clinton's success, for that matter, watching *The War Room* and laughing just like Brean and Motss laughed at the TV talk shows which were supposedly deconstructing the President's promotion strategies.

The War Room is the epitome of the hyperreal, i.e. the implosion of the real/fictional binary that we have been exploring in this book on various levels of generality. On the one hand, it promises to unveil the workings of the communication tactics and show us the process whereby Clinton's political image was constructed, while, at the same time, it succumbs to the classical rules of narrative construction that ensure a very coherent storyline, plausible and affective characters and, of course, a hymn of human initiative and goal-orientation. In this sense, its role is purely ideological in the most traditional fashion. The scene where Carville makes a speech to his stuff right before the Election Day is emblematic. Unable to hold back his tears, he teaches them a lesson in life, saying that combining 'love' and 'labour' is the greatest 'merger', while his take on luck is summed up as follows: 'Ben Hogan said "Golf is a game of luck, the more I practice, the luckier I get". The harder you work, the luckier you are.' Carville's is the perfect Hollywood tale: a romantic involvement and the pursuit of a goal that cannot be undercut by the vicissitudes of luck.⁵⁷ It is a perfect performance in front of a 'double' audience, namely those standing in front of him in the staff room and those who watch *The War Room* trying to understand 'why' and 'how' Clinton won the election.

The making of a documentary like *The War Room* in the early 1990s is fully aligned with the public fascination with what historian Neil Harris has dubbed the 'aesthetic of the operational',[58] i.e. the desire to look behind the scenes and see how something really works. Fiction filmmaking began catering to people's attraction to backstage politics from the 1970s with *The Candidate* as a typical example of this trend. By the 1990s, however, fictional accounts were no longer sufficient; we had to see the 'real' thing. D. A Pennebaker and Hegedus' work promises to show how Clinton's image was constructed and how that image was instrumental in his political victory. What is not openly stated is that *The War Room* is in fact an instance of 'meta-imaging', which is an act that displays and foregrounds the art and practice of political image construction.[59] Thus, *The War Room* is merely another communication strategy that functions simultaneously as 'a real depiction of the campaign and a highly planned and controlled rhetoric of image construction and maintenance.'[60] Within our current regime of truth, to remember Foucault's concept from Chapter 2, such a mixture of reality and fabrication is more than anticipated; it has become the staple of a multiply mediated social reality.

Conclusion

In this chapter I concentrated on two more aspects of *Wag the Dog*: its generic identity as a 'political film' and its depiction of political agency in the contemporary world. Both aspects elucidate two more facets of the cinema/reality complex. The first line of inquiry led me to a wider investigation of American political films and the difficulties that scholars have met in their attempt to construct these films as a concrete genre. Despite common claims that the lack of a distinct and popular 'political genre' is due to the films' formal inconsistencies, I argued that the core of this problem lies in the strong cultural verisimilitude that all political films inherently carry. Whereas the classical Hollywood genres, such as the musical, the western or melodrama, can provide stories that are allowed to depart from reality using generic norms and motivations, the political film is by nature grounded in the real world. Why by nature? Because a story about politics is primarily a story about making changes in the world, for better or for worse. And these changes not only tend to impact the lives of the many, but also reflect on the broader virtues of liberty and democracy. No matter how you may blend a political theme with a couple of funny lines or moments of breathtaking suspense, its ideological overtones still address the function of the political system in a democratic society. These close ties of the political movie with the real world and its outlook on how one could go about changing it could be regarded as potential sources of controversy within American society. This controversy, as I explained, is unwelcome by the industry and the audience alike. Occasionally, there can be ambitious attempts to discuss difficult issues of responsibility, ethics, power and justice but that could not be a weekly rendezvous at the movies.

The second line of thought in this section focused on the concept of agency and explored the way it is depicted in *Wag the Dog* and a number of other political narratives. In the former, I identified the tendency to distribute the action almost equally among individuals and objects, particularly the media. Levinson emphasized the reduced powers of the political figures by blatantly constraining the appearance of the President and his opponent while his protagonists emulated a battle between the hero as an active agent and a performer. Motss' faith in human initiative, imagination and acknowledgment of one's deeds was crashed by Brean's jaded acquiescence to the fact that political reality is not shaped by one's free will; rather it comprises a complex network of actors, both human and non-human, engaged in a communication process with codes of its own. In that process, whether something is true or not bears little informational value compared to how it may be embedded in the overall media frame.

With this model of agency in mind, I revisited the history of the American political film and suggested a new rationale for classifying the films about politics. Instead of following a strict chronological order and employing key historical events as markers, we could re-read the political narratives according to how they depict human agency vis-à-vis the political system or, more widely, society. From *The Candidate* to *The Ides of March*, one can identify multiple variations of human behaviour ranging from heroic patriotism to complete lack of power in an increasingly complex and impersonal political reality. Admittedly, however, films like *Wag the Dog* and *The Parallax View* belong rather to the minority, as most stories still cling to the individual as a rational agent with the potential to act upon reality. In fact, what is most striking about the tool of agency is how it unearths another point of convergence between fiction and non-fiction films, like *The War Room*. Whether claiming to depict real or fictional events, the device of the goal-oriented individual that can make a difference in the world remains by far the most popular device for representing the world around us.

Notes

1. Michael Coyne, *Hollywood Goes to Washington: American Politics on Screen* (London: Reaktion Books, 2008), 17.
2. I refer to Todorov's term, which I will elaborate shortly.
3. Andrew Sarris, *Politics and Cinema* (New York: Columbia University Press, 1978), 9.
4. For the broad spectrum of the political see Sarris, *Politics and Cinema*, Daniel Franklin, *Politics and Film: The political culture of film in the US* (Lanham, MD: Rowman & Littlefield Publishers, 2006), and Leonard Quart and Albert Auster, *American Film and Society since 1945: Third Edition, Revised and Expanded* (Westport, CT: Praeger, 2001).
5. Altman explains the distinction between an inclusive and exclusive list of films in the constitution of a generic corpus. Rick Altman, 'A Semantic/syntactic approach to film genre', in *Film Theory and Criticism: Introductory Readings*, ed. Leo Braudy and Marshall Cohen (New York: Oxford University Press, 1999), 27.
6. Steve Neale, *Genre and Hollywood* (London and New York: Routledge, 2000).
7. From now on the term 'political films' will be exclusively reserved for those which portray the American political scene, unless stated otherwise.
8. Coyne, *Hollywood Goes to Washington*, 9.
9. Altman, 'A semantic/syntactic approach to film genre'.
10. Steve Neale, 'Questions of genre', in *Film Genre Reader II*, ed. Barry Keith Grant (Texas: University Texas Press, 1995), 170.
11. Neale corroborates his argument by referring to Bordwell, Staiger and Thompson's work on Classical Hollywood cinema where they argued for the dual plot-line (romance/mission) in all classical films. Ibid., 171.
12. For structuralist approaches to other genres and most notably the western, see John G. Cawelti, *Six-Gun Mystique* (Ohio: Bowling Green University Popular Press, 1970), Will Wright, *Sixguns & Society: A Structural Study of the Western* (Berkeley: University of California Press, 1975) and Jim Kitses, *Horizons West: Anthony Mann, Budd Boetticher, Sam Peckinpah: Studies of Authorship Within the Western* (London: Thames and Hudson, 1969).
13. Terry Christensen, *Reel Politics: American Political Movies from Birth of a Nation to Platoon* (Oxford and New York: Blackwell, 1987), 3.
14. Ibid., 3.
15. Altman, 'A Semantic/syntactic approach to film genre,' 29.
16. Ibid., 36.
17. Indicatively, I refer to the reviews at http://essexoutletcinemas.blogspot.

com/2006/10/man-of-year.html [Accessed 22 November 2011] and http://www.popentertainment.com/manoftheyear.htm [Accessed 22 November 2011].

18. The review was entitled '"Man of the Year" is a very good political thriller/comedy that will suffer at the box office because of its misleading marketing campaign'. http://www.imdb.com/title/tt0483726/reviews [Accessed 22 November 2011].
19. Neale, 'Questions of genre', 160.
20. Apart from Coyne and Christensen, it is worth referring to Ian Scott's book *American Politics in Hollywood Film*, where we also evidence the contradiction that political films are alike and thus could be grouped as a separate genre and, yet, at the same time this grouping seems either impossible or incomplete at best. Ian Scott, *American Politics in Hollywood Film* (Edinburgh: Edinburgh University Press, 2000).
21. Todorov in Neale, 'Questions of genre', 160–1.
22. Phillip L. Gianos, *Politics and Politicians in American Film* (Westport, CT: Praeger, 1998) and Linda Alkana, 'The Absent President: Mr. Smith, The Candidate, and Bulworth', in *Hollywood's White House: The American Presidency in Film and History*, ed. Peter C. Rollins and John E. O'Connor (Lexington, KY: University of Kentucky Press, 2003).
23. Brian Neve, 'Frames of presidential and candidate politics in American films of the 1990s', *The Public* Vol. 7 (2000): 24.
24. I am referring to the script of *The Candidate*, which, according to Christensen's sources, got a green light from Senator John Tunney, as both writer Jeremy Larner and director Michael Ritchie had worked on his campaign in 1970 in California.
25. Scott, *American Politics in Hollywood Film*, 159.
26. Coyne dedicates his conclusion to the anticipatory qualities of the political genre. Coyne, *Hollywood Goes to Washington*, 190-9.
27. David Bordwell, Janet Staiger, and Kristin Thompson, *The Classical Hollywood Cinema: Film Style and Mode of Production to 1960* (New York: Routledge, 1985).
28. Thomas Elsaesser, 'The pathos of failure. American Films in the 70s: Notes on the unmotivated hero', *Monogram*, 6 (1975).
29. Ibid.
30. Alkana, 'The Absent President', 194.
31. Thomas Elsaesser began to explore a new type of hero in films, such as *The Truman Show* (1998), *Fight Club* (1999), *The Sixth Sense* (1999), *Memento* (2000), *Mulholland Dr.* (2001), *Minority Report* (2003), *The Butterfly Effect* (2004). Thomas Elsaesser, 'The Mind-Game Film', in *Puzzle Films*, ed. Warren Buckland (Oxford: Blackwell, 2009).
32. See also Chapter 2.
33. See Chapter 1 for the narrative significance of the final shot.

34 See Chapters 1 and 2.
35 Bruno Latour, *Science in Action: How to Follow Scientists and Engineers Through Society* (Cambridge, MA: Harvard University Press, 1987).
36 Bruno Latour, *Re-assembling the social: An Introduction to Actor-Network-Theory* (New York: Oxford University Press, 2005).
37 Ibid., 71.
38 Cynthia Weber raises a similar argument about the problem of tracing an author in *Wag the Dog*, viewing it through the theory of social constructivism in international relations. Even though I agree with some of her observations, I believe that her choice to attribute 'agency' to 'tales and practices' instead of 'individuals', as she notes, does not offer us a definitive solution to the problem of 'intersubjective' agency, as actor-network theory does. Cynthia Weber, *International Relations Theory: A Critical Introduction* (New York: Routledge, 2001).
39 Luhmann's book *The Reality of the Mass Media* (2000) was first published in German in 1996 and consists of a lecture on the topic delivered in Düsseldorf in 1994.
40 See also Chapter 2.
41 Niklas Luhmann, *The Reality of the Mass Media* (Stanford: Stanford University Press, 2000), 5.
42 Luhmann's theories have been widely criticised by Jurgen Habermas and other Marxist thinkers. Indicatively see Jürgen Habermas, *The Philosophical Discourse of Modernity: Twelve Lectures (Studies in Contemporary German Social Thought)* (Cambridge, MA: MIT Press, 1993).
43 Christensen, *Reel Politics*; Brian Neve, *Film and Politics in America: A Social Tradition* (London: Routledge, 1992); Scott, *American Politics in Hollywood Film*; Harry Keyishian, *Screening Politics; The Politician in American Movies, 1931–2001* (Lanham, MD: Scarecrow Press, 2003); Peter Rollins and John O'Connor, *Hollywood's White House: The American Presidency in Film and History* (Lexington, KY: University Press of Kentucky, 2003); Coyne, *Hollywood Goes to Washington*.
44 Coyne, *Hollywood Goes to Washington*, 19–40.
45 Ibid., 32.
46 See note 42.
47 Sarris, *Politics and Cinema*.
48 Christensen notes 'But in *The Candidate* the system was bigger than the individual. The process itself dominates, and individuals were swept along by it.' Christensen, *Reel Politics*, 131.
49 Bordwell, Staiger, and Thompson, *The Classical Hollywood Cinema*.

50 Christensen, *Reel Politics*.
51 Stella Bruzzi notes, 'At a White House dinner to commemorate the Hollywood version of *Primary Colors*, Bill Clinton invited John Travolta, who in the film plays his visual doppelganger Jack Stanton, to impersonate him for the assembled guests. Travolta declined, but both Clinton's action and the accuracy of Travolta's rendition of Clinton's mannerisms in Nichols' film demonstrate the corrosion of the distinction between the real and the performed.' Stella Bruzzi, *New Documentary: A Critical Introduction* (Abingdon: Routledge, 2006), 175.
52 Suzanne Lezotte, 'Phedon Papamichael, ASC, Lenses "The Ides of March"', *Panavision*, October 7, 2011, http://www.panavision.com/spotlight/phedon-papamichael-asc-lenses-ides-march.
53 Apart from the references to the Clinton sex scandal, the characters also refer to other well-known political incidents, such as Lyndon Johnson's words 'I just want to hear him deny it' or the question about the death penalty that was addressed to Michael Dukakis during his campaign.
54 Robert Stam, Robert Burgoyne, and Sandy Flitterman-Lewis, *New Vocabularies in Film Semiotics: Structuralism, Poststructuralism and Beyond* (London and New York: Routledge, 1993), 154.
55 For an extensive analysis of the militarist metaphors and language in the film, see J. Parry-Giles and T. Parry-Giles, 'Meta-Imaging, The War Room, and the Hyperreality of U.S. Politics', *Journal of Communication* 49 (1999).
56 Ibid., 33.
57 Note how, according to Bordwell et al., the key characteristics of the classical narration include the double plotline, i.e. intertwining the formation of the heterosexual couple with the accomplishment of a mission, while the role of chance is only peripheral and allowed to step forward only in specific genres like melodrama and comedy. Bordwell, Staiger, and Thompson, *The Classical Hollywood Cinema*.
58 In David Haven Blake, 'Hollywood, Impersonation, and Presidential Celebrity in the 1990s', in *Hollywood's White House: The American Presidency in Film and History*, ed. Peter C. Rollins and John E. O'Connor (Lexington: University Press of Kentucky, 2003), 330.
59 Parry-Giles and Parry-Giles, 'Meta-Imaging', 29.
60 Ibid., 30.

Conclusion

Wag the Dog and its Universe

My study on film and reality using *Wag the Dog* as a pivotal case in the history of cinema is nearing its end. In these concluding pages I would like to revisit the terms and the concepts, the observations and the arguments that stemmed from the close analysis of the film and the surrounding reality in order to provide the reader with an overview as well as a blueprint of this complex relation. To that end, I would like to return to Souriau's grand scheme to define the principles of filmology, which I presented in Chapter 1, and borrow his typology of the 'seven levels of existence' in the structure of the filmic universe. As I reframe my own findings into Souriau's levels, I hope to shed light into the universe of *Wag the Dog* and its bearing on the state of cinema in the current age.

The afilmic reality. The external reality that exists beyond the filmic text is impossible to contain within a single description, as the multitude of elements that comprise it is essentially infinite. As we try to understand the real world, however, we are bound to identify certain elements that stand out, such as specific events or personages, and then to organize them into a single narrative with specific causal, spatial and temporal characteristics. In my attempt to describe the afilmic reality of *Wag the Dog*, I was primarily guided by the temporal nature of certain facts, tracing events and issues in the real world that had appeared before the making of the film. Thus, I discussed the aesthetics of the Persian Gulf War, the 24-hour live TV coverage of the missile attacks, the public relations campaign against the Iraqis and the reporting methods that pervaded in the coverage of that war. Moreover, I noted a number of developments in the communication strategy of the White House from the Nixon administration onwards, while I presented the case of Oliver North as emblematic of the mythology of the 'war hero' in the American political culture. After an admittedly selective look into the afilmic reality that preceded the film's screening, I turned to the afilmic elements, the reviews and the media references, which surfaced shortly after the screening, noting a number of ambivalent commentaries. However, the time during which people could ponder upon the film's message on its own right was unexpectedly brief; the outbreak of a major afilmic event, the Lewinsky scandal, and the similarities of the real events with those depicted in the film's diegesis caused the barriers between the real and the reel world to be definitively challenged. From then on *Wag the Dog* would enter the afilmic reality as a template, i.e. as an interpretative framework for evaluating or even prescribing political events. Yet, the transformation of a filmic element into an afilmic one is not unique to *Wag the Dog*. The entire tradition of high-concept filmmaking has migrated into the real world providing formulas, ideas and tips on how to handle real situations. To be precise, high-concept filmmaking generates exchanges between the filmic and the afilmic on two counts; on the one hand, high-concept films are designed to impact the lives of the spectators well beyond the movie theatre by encouraging them to adopt fads and fashions in their everyday life.[1] On the other hand, high-concept filmmaking lends its strategies to news broadcasting leading the media professionals to treat afilmic elements as if they were filmic. Describing, ordering and, ultimately, selling reality as if it were fiction establishes a new regime of truth in contemporary global societies.

The profilmic reality. The profilmic reality of *Wag the Dog* is fairly easy to describe since Levinson mostly relied on live-action footage. In other words, the profilmic reality contains all the actors and the settings that stood in front of the camera and were recorded by analogue means. It also contains Levinson and his crew, who made a brief appearance, as I we saw in Figures 1.9–1.10. The difference, however, between the profilmic presence of De Niro and Levinson is that the former was filmed in order to be later transformed into a diegetic element, while the latter would cling to his afilmic existence. A complication arises when we try to classify the status of the TV images that pervade throughout the film or even the surveillance images that appear on various occasions. In fact, the difficulty concerns the entire notion of mediation and its representation on the screen. My suggestion would be to acknowledge a doubly framed profilmic reality in the cases when a person or an object appears as a mediated level of reality. For instance, the news anchorman who appears on TV poses, in fact, twice in front of the camera lens; first as the actor and then as anchorman. Similarly, when we see De Niro pass through security checks, the film emulates the profilmic reality by showing us the actor as raw material recorded by the surveillance camera.

The filmographic reality. At this level, we begin to address the actual film, i.e. the celluloid, on which the profilmic events were recorded. Souriau includes in this category the editing of the film, given that at his time the editing processes involved the cutting of the actual celluloid. Nowadays, we would need to acknowledge the collaboration of computer technology for the shaping of the filmographic reality, i.e. the final version of the film. In the case of *Wag the Dog* computers were certainly employed for the editing of the film, while various modalities such as electronic and digital images were all incorporated in the digital material before finally being printed back on celluloid. In other words, the filmographic reality of *Wag the Dog*, like most of the films today, includes not only its existence as an analogue medium, but also the digital version that was created during post-production and was employed for the release of the film on DVD or other media formats.

The filmophanic reality. This is the type of reality that lights up on the screen during the projection of the film in the theatre. The parameters of this level can be distinguished into two subcategories. First, there is filmophanic reality in the widest sense, which is contingent upon the characteristics of projection. Second, there is screen reality,[2] which contains the forms of the filmic image that a spectator witnesses during the screening. Among these forms we could include mise-en-scène cues, framing choices, camera placement and shot duration.[3] Therefore, the filmophanic reality in *Wag the Dog* entails all those stylistic devices that we discussed in Chapter 1, such as high-angle framing, zooming shots, shaky camera movements and the prominence of objects in the mise-en-scène. Moreover, under this category we would include the presence of multiple modalities, varying from TV shots and surveillance images to digital inserts, such as the kitten in the hands of the Albanian girl. The different filmic textures of these images illustrate how digital technology can easily combine different image sources on a single filmographic material.

The diegesis. At this level we enter the world of fiction where reality appears only as direct or indirect reference. The story world in *Wag the Dog* is concerned with politics and the media. As far as politics is concerned, the diegesis clings to a high sense of cultural verisimilitude, presenting the plot in a realistic and plausible fashion. Hyperbolic as the main premise about the Albanian war may be, the settings, the technology and the media activity resonate with contemporary developments in the political scene. When it comes to the media, *Wag the Dog* addresses head-on all the fine nuances of Souriau's filmic universe, problematizing the distinction between its diverse levels. For instance, we repeatedly hear Brean question the ingredients of afilmic reality, arguing that there is no way of knowing whether something really happened or not. Moreover, we see him and Motss fabricate reality as if it were a teaser or a pageant. In the world that these characters inhabit, the afilmic/filmic distinction no longer holds. In the same vein, the making and the broadcasting of the fake news video elaborates on the impact of the digital technology on profilmic, filmographic and filmophanic realities.[4] During the shooting scene, analysed in depth in Chapter 2, we notice how the role of the profilmic elements changes at the age of the digital. They only needed an actress to pose for the camera in front of a blue screen, since all the other elements would be 'punched in' later during post-production. In the case of CGI images or the photomontage that takes place in the control room, we realize that the level of profilmic reality is obviated while the creation occurs at the filmographic level, which is no longer limited to the celluloid. Even though I could not possibly know how Souriau would evaluate the passage from the analogue to the digital, my sense is that his taxonomy is spacious enough to accommodate the technological innovations that have always been part and parcel of the life of cinema. Therefore, if we accept pixels and computer software alongside celluloid still as the filmographic level of the filmic universe today, we might have to compromise our faith in the profilmic but not necessarily in the afilmic. The relation between the filmographic and the afilmic reality becomes more contingent but it is by no means eliminated altogether. Besides, the problem with the fake news video did not lie in the fact that its images came from stock libraries; instead, the problem lay in the intentions of its makers to deceive the public and in the dissemination of the video tagged as live footage. And this brings me to the other major theme highlighted in the diegesis, namely the role of immediacy. The notion of immediacy became pertinent in my study in relation to realistic conventions of representation, on the one hand, and the liveness of TV broadcasting, on the other. The aesthetics of the fake video relied on the classical sense of realism that ordained the frame to operate as a transparent window on to the world and the digital technology to create a coherent and continuous spatiotemporal setting. Thus, it became evident that, despite any changes at the filmographic level (digital or analogue), the screen reality might come off just the same. Finally, the film's diegesis emphasized the impact of immediacy that comes with the 24-hour live television. This aspect of immediacy, contrary to all the other aforementioned elements, does not seem to pertain, at first glance, to our traditional conception of cinema. As Andrew's mellifluous description puts it,

And that rule is that cinema's voltage depends on delay and slippage, what I dub the *décalage* at the heart of the medium and of each film between 'here and there' as well as 'now and then.' This French term connotes discrepancy in space and deferral or jump in time. At the most primary level, the film image leaps from present to past, since what is edited and shown was filmed at least days, weeks or months earlier.[5]

Yet, the heart of the medium started changing pace from 1990s onwards. Thanks to the widespread use of video, dvds and, now, the internet, films spread massively and rapidly, compelling Andrew to argue that in the phase of 'global cinema' electronic distribution may eventually obviate all delay and 'the attendant experience of *décalage*.'[6] Thus, *Wag the Dog*'s diegesis and its dramatic emphasis on immediacy and speed draw our attention to the cataclysmic changes that would affect all media, old and new, in the age of synergy, digital convergence and conglomerate distribution networks.

The spectatorial events. The impact of *Wag the Dog* on the spectators after its initial screening could be differentiated according to both temporal and geographical criteria. If one viewed the film before the Lewinsky scandal, they would be inclined to assign to the diegetic elements a rather indeterminate reference, according to Branigan's description of a fictional reading, as I explained in Chapter 1. That inclination would result mostly from afilmic elements, such as the institutional tag of the 'fiction film', and diegetic cues that indicate an indirect relation to the real world. Drawing on past knowledge from historical and political events, the average viewer would be free to interpret the story world according to their personal judgement, discovering overt or covert connections to external reality. Certain filmophanic elements, such as the zooming shots, the camera placement and the prominence of TV sets in the décor, could momentarily baffle them as to the nature, fictional or non-fictional, of certain images but the overall impression would still veer towards fiction. However, the news of the scandal as well as the peculiar timing of the bombings over the following months would change the interpretative framework of the film. The coincidence of the afilmic elements with the diegetic ones that had preceded could alter the direction of the reading of the film, triggering a different set of expectations. Apart from the fact that several people and actions from the story world would be assigned a more determinate reference (the President = Clinton and Firefly girl = Lewinsky), the audience could look at *Wag the Dog*, searching for evidence that would help them assess the evolving political reality. This shift of focus from the past (what happened) to the future (what might happen) was most evident in the reading of the film by people outside the United States. Whether you were a reader of *Le Monde* in France or a Serbian living in Kosovo, the film was likely to provoke mixed reactions and anticipations regarding the significance of the film for things to come.[7]

The creatorial level. Was all that ingeniously planned by Levinson and his collaborators? Yes and no. Their reactions to the outbreak of the Lewinsky scandal clearly showed that they were all taken aback by the similarities between fact and fiction. Yet, Levinson's instinct about the impact of television, and by extension all mediation, on external reality was right on target from the very start of his career. As my close look into some of his key films demonstrated, Levinson was deeply concerned about how the images of life disseminated through TV could change life itself forever. From *Diner* to *Avalon* and from *The Man of the Year* to *Poliwood*, he explored the impact of television, shifting his focus from the everyday life of middle-class Americans to the foremost electoral process, the presidential elections. In *Wag the Dog*, Levinson drew attention to the creatorial level through his brief extradiegetic presence, while he also made himself present in those group meetings when the camera lens randomly zoomed in on the characters and the abrupt cutting indicated a strong non-diegetic narrator. Given how difficult it is, by and large, to measure whether a filmmaker achieves his goals and gets his message across, *Wag the Dog* constitutes a rare case when it is fairly safe to assume that Levinson and his collaborators were both talented and lucky enough to make a film with such lasting effect.

Some final thoughts

The examination of the universe of *Wag the Dog* à la Souriau as well as the entire study of the film in the preceding chapters has allowed us to witness the intricate play between cinema and reality that takes on multiple forms and shapes. On many occasions it was difficult to separate the filmic from the afilmic, the fact from fiction, as the two realms kept relentlessly feeding off each other. So is this a new situation? Has *Wag the Dog* as a film and as a media event signaled a new phase in the relation between cinema and reality? I suggest we return to the concept of the 'digital' and see how we can draw some answers.

In Chapter 3, I suggested that the digital might prove useful as a metaphor for the evolving relation between cinema and reality. Two emblematic operations of digital technology, the process of negation and the uniformity of the single numerical code, could help us conceptualize both the workings of the narrative and the function of the film in the political context soon afterwards. On the one hand, the technical capacity of computer technology to generate images without any profilmic reality facilitates the prospects for pure simulation, for iconicity for the sake of it. *Wag the Dog* illustrated this process most emphatically in the production of the fake Albanian war and then spread suspicion all around the world about the possibility that President Clinton's actions against Sudan, Afghanistan and later Iraq, were also based on 'simulated' justifications. Most importantly, however, it spread the suspicion that we will never be able to tell the difference between a real cause and a fake one, as if they were both made up from a single code. In other words, in this day and age fact and fiction, afilmic and filmic elements, end up on the same level of 'reality' constructed, by and large, by the media.[8] Yet, is this constitutive hybridity of cinema and reality in contemporary mass mediated social reality a 'new thing'? Again, the long-standing theories of the digital could offer a point of comparison, since the aspect of 'newness' has been the utmost bone of contention for them over the past couple of decades. Even though I could not possibly present a similarly exhaustive account in these closing lines, I would like to venture some general thoughts.

First and foremost, the current media landscape is admittedly different from what it was during the time that cinema made its first steps. From the vaudeville theatres, the kinetoscopes and the Nickelodeons to the iPod screens, the moving images have run a long course engaging people's lives in numerous and diverse ways. The dominance of computer technology from 1990s onwards altered irrevocably several aspects of the cinematic medium, establishing an enormous manipulability at the level of production, an unprecedented degree of convergence and synergy at the level of distribution and an increased level of interactivity at the level of exhibition.[9] Yet, the question remains; have these new technical means *radically* changed the relation between cinema and reality? Haven't the filmic elements always infiltrated reality in both planned but also unforeseen manners? Remember the example of the Hollywood industry during World War II. At the time, feature films, newsreels and documentaries were the key sources of information for millions of Americans. Never before and never since has Hollywood worked so closely with the American government for the mobilization of public opinion against the foreign threat and the need for the United States to, first, get involved in the world conflict and, then, fight it until the final victory. Patriotic tales and heroic battles flooded the screens in all types of formats; from Frank Capra's documentary series *Why We Fight* (1942–5) to hundreds of musicals and war films that fuelled the collective imagination in America. The filmic and the afilmic elements kept crossing paths, as Hollywood actresses entertained real soldiers, while actors, like Tyrone Power and Clark Gable, enlisted in the army. The case of World War II testifies how closely interwoven the lives of fact and fiction have always been, making it impossible to consider one without the other. Thus, should we conclude that everything that we discussed about *Wag the Dog* in this book is merely 'business as usual'? My answer is no. Trapped though I am in the same quandary with every theorist of the digital, namely the difficulty of defining the 'newness' of the phenomenon in hand, I am more inclined to argue that *Wag the Dog* is indeed invaluable for understanding the relation between cinema and reality across time by addressing different questions for each phase in the history of the medium. And this is the ultimate paradox of this study on film and reality. On the one hand, we are drawn into the textual and contextual particularities of Levinson's film for the way they disclose the workings of visual culture in the current age. On the other, we begin to challenge several of our assumptions about the ways the relation between cinema and reality has functioned at different historical junctures. By analysing the filmic/afilmic elements as they developed in this specific case, we are encouraged to trace continuities and similarities with other pivotal eras when cinema performed a highly influential role in its social and political context. Yet, I will not evade the issue of 'newness' by arguing for continuities and discontinuities, no matter how substantial this argument may be. Drawing again on the digital analogy, *Wag the Dog* may appear to simply magnify, multiply and intensify the film/reality interactions of the past, and, in this sense, it may not appear to amount to an entirely new phenomenon.[10] And for some thinkers a change in *degree* may not be as important as a change in *kind*.[11] Yet, my position is that the accumulative effects of the changes in degree lead, in fact, to a change in kind that has yet to be fully perceived and acknowledged. So far, we could describe the specifics of this particular case and we could even go as far as the stage of the metaphor in order to codify those specifics into meaningful patterns.[12] I am afraid that only hindsight or history could allow us to identify whether the changes in the cinema/reality complex in the era of *Wag the Dog* indicate a broader epistemological shift in Western society or whether the film merely stands for the contemporary version of Plato's cave.

Notes

1. One could argue that all films potentially bring on changes in the real lives of spectators by affecting directly or indirectly the way they feel, think or behave. The particularity of high-concept films, however, is that they are meant to infiltrate the lives of the audience in a way that is more directly related to filmic elements. For instance, I might become more tolerant towards immigrants if I watch Michael Winterbottom's *In this World* (2002) but it is less likely that I will identify this change as a 'Winterbottom effect'. In contrast, if I buy toys that portray the characters of a film or if I dress in T-shirts of my favourite blockbuster, I allow the filmic elements to keep on living in the real world.
2. Souriau uses the term 'écranique' for this subdivision of filmophanic reality. Etienne Souriau, 'La structure de l'univers filmique et le vocabulaire de la filmologie', *Revue Internationale de Filmologie* 7–8 (1951): 236–7.
3. Despite coining the term filmophanic/screen reality three decades before the formulation of more specific narrative terms, we easily accommodate at this level all those elements that David Bordwell has classified as 'film style' with the exception of editing, which would have to be included in the filmographic level, if we were to remain faithful to Souriau's rationale. David Bordwell, *Narration in the Fiction Film* (London: Routledge, 1985).
4. Even though the news video is not a feature film that would open in the theatres, the operations entailed in its making apply to the filmmaking process and allow us to draw the parallels with Souriau's concepts for the filmic universe.
5. Dudley Andrew, 'Time Zones and Jetlag: The Flows and Phases of World Cinema', in *World Cinemas, Transnational Perspectives*, ed. Natasa Durovicova and Kathleen Newman (New York: Routledge, 2010), 60.
6. Andrew, 'Time Zones', 81.
7. Klaus Dodds, *Geopolitics: a Very Short Introduction* (Oxford: Oxford University Press, 2007), 20.
8. A very important clarification is in order regarding the use of the word 'constructed'. Depending on 'who' we believe is responsible for this 'construction' and 'why', alters considerably our political, ideological and, ultimately, philosophical viewpoint on humanity. If we hold that the media act as capitalist enterprises that peddle false consciousness into the public in order to generate profits and perpetuate the status quo, then clearly we align ourselves with the Marxist theories that describe their own solutions to the problem of 'construction' and the transcendence required for making a better world. If, on the other hand, we approach the media as impersonal systems that function in ways that exceed human consciousness and deliberateness, then systems theories, like those

presented in Chapter 4, are more likely to offer convincing, if more pessimistic, explanations. See Chapter 4, n. 35, 36, 39, 41 and 42.

9 Philip Rosen, *Change Mummified: Cinema, Historicity, Theory* (Minneapolis: Minnesota University Press, 2001), 319–49.

10 Here I am paraphrasing Maureen Turim who argued that 'Digital artmaking has magnified, multiplied, and intensified the codes of analogy'. Maureen Turim, 'Artisanal prefigurations of the digital: animating realities, collage effects, and theories of image manipulation', *Wide Angle* 21, 1 (1999): 51.

11 Philip Rosen, *Change Mummified*, 231.

12 Rudolf Schmitt, 'Systematic Metaphor Analysis as a Method of Qualitative Research', *The Qualitative Report* 10, 2 (2005): 360.

Bibliography

Adams, Kathleen, Maryanne Murray Buechner, Jon Goldstein, Tam Gray, Anita Hamilton, Nadya Labi, Michele Orecklin and Alain L. Sanders. 'Wag the Clinton.' *Time Magazine*, Notebook, 151, 4, 2 February 1998. http://www.time.com/time/magazine/article/0,9171,987767,00.html [Accessed 30 May 1999]

Alkana, Linda. 'The Absent President: Mr. Smith, The Candidate, and Bulworth'. In Peter C. Rollins and John E. O'Connor (eds), *Hollywood's White House: The American Presidency in Film and History*, 193–205. Lexington, KY: University of Kentucky Press, 2003.

Altman, Rick. 'A Semantic/syntactic approach to film genre'. In *Film Theory and Criticism: Introductory Readings*, Leo Braudy and Marshall Cohen (eds), 630–41. New York: Oxford University Press, 1999.

Andersen, R. 'Oliver North and the News'. In P. Dahlgren and C. Sparks (eds), *Journalism and Popular Culture,*. London: Sage, 1993.

Andrew, Dudley. *Concepts in Film Theory*. New York: Oxford University Press, 1984.

—'Time Zones and Jetlag: The Flows and Phases of World Cinema'. In Natasa Durovicova and Kathleen Newman (eds), *World Cinemas, Transnational Perspectives*, 59–89. New York: Routledge, 2010.

—*What Cinema Is!* Malden, MA: Wiley-Blackwell, 2010.

Andrew, Dudley and Hervé Joubert-Laurencin (eds). *Opening Bazin: Postwar Film Theory and Its Afterlife*. New York: Oxford University Press, 2011.

Ansen, David. 'Wag the dog'. *Newsweek*, 22 December 1997. http://newsweek.com/nw-srv/tnw/today/as/mv/mv_w.htm [Accessed 17 April 2000].

Arnheim, Rudolf. *Film as Art*. Berkeley: University of California Press, 1957.

Atkins, Stephen ed. *The 9/11 Encyclopedia*. Westport, CT: Praeger, 1998.

Bacevich, Andrew J. ed. *The Long War: a New History of U.S. National Security Policy since World War II*. New York: Columbia University Press, 2007.

Balász, Béla. *Early Film Theory: Visible Man and The Spirit of Film*. Erica Carter ed. New York: Berghahn Books, 2010.

Baudrillard, Jean. *La guerre du Golfe n' a pas eu lieu*. Paris: Galilée, 1991.

—*Simulacra and simulation*. Ann Arbor: The University of Michigan Press, 1994.

—*The Gulf War Did Not Take Place*. Bloomington: Indiana University Press, 1995.

Baum, Matthew. 'Sex, Lies and War: How soft news brings foreign policy to the inattentive public'. *American Political Science Review* 96 (March 2002): 91–109.

—*Soft News Goes to War: Public Opinion and American Foreign Policy in the New Media Age*. Princeton: Princeton University Press, 2005.

Bazin, André. *What is Cinema?* Vol. I. Berkeley: University of California Press, [1967] 2005.
—*What is Cinema?* Vol. II. Berkeley: University of California Press, [1971] 2005.
Beinhart, Larry. *American Hero*. New York: Pantheon Books, 1993.
Belton, John. 'Digital Cinema: A False Revolution'. *October* 100 (2002): 98–114.
Bennett, Lance W. *News: the Politics of Illusion*. New York: Longman, 1996.
Berlin, Joey. 'White House Sex Scandal Cheers Dustin Hoffmann'. *Hollywood*, 3 February 2000. www.hollywood.com/news/berlin/02-02-98/ [Accessed 15 March 1999]
Black, Joel. *The Reality Effect: Film Culture and the Graphic Imperative*. New York, London: Routledge, 2002.
Blake, David Haven. 'Hollywood, Impersonation, and Presidential Celebrity in the 1990s'. In Peter C. Rollins and John E. O'Connor (eds), *Hollywood's White House: The American Presidency in Film and History*, 320–32. Lexington: University Press of Kentucky, 2003.
Blumenfeld, Samuel. 'Trop gentil pour être subversif'. *Monde*, 30 April 1998.
Bolter, Jay David and Richard Grusin. *Remediation: Understanding New Media*. Cambridge, MA: MIT Press, 1999.
Bolter, Jay David. 'The Desire for Transparency in an Era of Hybridity'. *Leonardo* 39, 2 (2006): 109–11.
Bordwell, David. *Narration in the Fiction Film*. London: Routledge, 1985.
—*The Way Hollywood Tells It: Story and Style in Modern Times*. Berkeley: University of California Press, 2006.
Bordwell, David, Janet Staiger, and Kristin Thompson. *The Classical Hollywood Cinema: Film Style and Mode of Production to 1960*. New York: Routledge, 1985.
Bourdon, Jérôme. 'Live television is still alive: on television as an unfulfilled promise'. *Media Culture Society* 22 (2000): 531–56.
Brahney, Kathleen J. 'U.S. Air strikes against Afghanistan, Sudan: Mixed Views on Washington's Action'. *USIA*, 21 August 1998. www.usia.gov/admin/005/wwwh8821.html [Accessed 30 May 1999]
Branigan, Edward. *Narrative Comprehension and Film*. London and New York: Routledge, 1992.
Bruzzi, Stella. *New Documentary: A Critical Introduction*. Abingdon, Oxon: Routledge, 2006.
Buckland, Warren. 'Between science fact and fiction: Spielberg's digital dinosaurs, possible worlds, and the new aesthetic realism'. *Screen* 40, 2 (1999): 177–92.
Carr, Howie. 'Obama's free ride over'. *Boston Herald*, 5 October 2012. http://www.bostonherald.com/news/columnist/view/20221005obamas_free_ride_over/srvc=home&position=3 [Accessed 1 May 2013]
Carroll, Noël. 'From Real to Reel: Entangled in Non-Fiction Film'. *Philosophic Exchange*, 14, (1983): 5–46.

—*Theorizing the Moving Image*. New York: Cambridge University Press, 1996.

Cawelti, John. *Six-Gun Mystique*. Ohio: Bowling Green University Popular Press, 1970.

Christensen, Terry. *Reel Politics: American Political Movies from Birth of a Nation to Platoon*. Oxford and New York: Blackwell, 1987.

Cohen, Richard. 'But is it a matter for the law?' *Washington Post*, 23 January 1998.

Coyne, Michael. *Hollywood Goes to Washington: American Politics on Screen*. London: Reaktion Books, 2008.

Cubitt, Sean. 'Phalke, Méliès, and special effects today'. *Wide Angle* 21, 1 (1999): 115–29.

Dawson, Ashley and Malini Johar Schueller. *Exceptional State: Contemporary U.S. Culture and the New Imperialism*. Durham and London: Duke University Press, 2007.

Der Derian, James. 'Virtually Wagging the Dog'. *Theory & Event* 2, 1 (1998).

—'The war of networks'. *Theory & Event* 5, 4 (2002).

Dillard, James Price and Michael Pfau. *The Persuasion Handbook: Developments in Theory and Practice*. Thousand Oaks, CA: Sage Publications, 2002.

Dixon, Wheeler Winston. 'The Digital Domain: Image Mesh and Manipulation in Hyperreal Cinema/Video'. *Film Criticism* 20, 1/2 (1995): 55–66.

Doane, Mary Ann. 'Information, Crisis, Catastrophe'. In Patricia Mellencamp ed. *Logics of Television: Essays in Cultural Criticism*. Bloomington: Indiana University Press, 1990.

Dodds, Klaus. *Geopolitics: a Very Short Introduction*. Oxford: Oxford University Press, 2007.

Edelman, Murray. *Constructing the Political Spectacle*. Chicago: University of Chicago Press, 1988.

—*The Politics of Misinformation*. Cambridge: Cambridge University Press, 2001.

Eisenstein, Sergei. *Film Form: Essays in Film Theory*. Translated by Jay Leyda. New York: Meridian Books, 1957.

Elsaesser, Thomas. 'Between Style and Ideology'. *Monogram* 3 (1972): 2–10.

—'The pathos of failure. American Films in the 70s: Notes on the unmotivated hero'. *Monogram*, 6 (1975): 13–19.

—'Subject Positions, Speaking Positions: From Holocaust, our Hitler, and Heimat to Shoah and Schindler's List'. In Vivian Sobchack ed. *The Persistence of History: Cinema, Television and the Modern Event*. New York: Routledge, 1996.

—'Digital Cinema: delivery, event, time'. In Thomas Elsaesser and Kay Hoffmann (eds), Cinema Futures: Cain, Abel or Cable? The Screen Arts in the Digital Age, 201–22. Amsterdam: Amsterdam University Press, 1998.

—'Louis Lumière – the cinema's first virtualist'. In Thomas Elsaesser and Kay Hoffmann (eds), Cinema Futures: Cain, Abel or Cable? The Screen Arts in the Digital Age, 45–61. Amsterdam: Amsterdam University Press, 1998.

—*Early Cinema: Space Frame Narrative*. London: BFI, 1990.

—'History Memory Identity and the Moving Image: One Train May be Hiding Another'. In edited by Linda Belau and Petar Ramadanovic (eds), *Topologies of Trauma: Essays on the Limit of Knowledge and Memory*, 61–72. New York: Other Press, 2002.

—'Early Film History and Multi-media: An Archaeology of Possible Futures?' In Wendy Hui Kyong Chun and Thomas Keenan (eds), *New Media, Old Media: A History and Theory Reader*, 13–25. New York: Routledge, 2005.

—'The Mind-Game Film'. In *Puzzle Films*, edited by Warren Buckland, 13–41. Oxford: Blackwell, 2009.

—'The Cinema in the 21st Century. Art-Form or a Form of Life?' Lecture at Goethe-University, Frankfurt am Main, November 6, 2012.

Elsaesser, Thomas and Malte Hagener. *Film Theory: An Introduction through the Senses*. London and New York: Routledge, 2010.

Ferro, Marc. *Cinema and History*. Detroit: Wayne State University Press, 1988.

Fetveit, Arild. 'Reality TV in the digital era: a paradox in visual culture?' *Media Culture Society* 21 (1999): 787–804.

Franklin, Daniel. *Politics and Film: The political culture of film in the US*. Lanham, MD: Rowman & Littlefield Publishers, 2006.

Gamson, William A. and Modigliani, Andre. 'The changing culture of affirmative action'. *Research in Political Sociology* 3 (1987): 137–77.

Gaylard, Gerard. 'The Postmodern archaic: the return of the real in digital virtuality'. *Postmodern Culture* 15, 1 (2004). http://muse.jhu.edu/journals/postmodern_culture/v015/15.1gaylard.html [Accessed 8 April 2008].

Georges, Pierre. 'Bande-Annonce'. *Monde*, February 21, 1998.

Gianos, Phillip L. *Politics and Politicians in American Film*. Westport, CT: Praeger, 1998.

Good, Howard (ed.). *Journalism Ethics goes to the Movies*. Lanham, MD: Rowman & Littlefield, 2008.

Greene, Ray. 'Wag The Dog'. *Box Office Magazine*, 25 December 1997. http://www.boxofficemagazine.com/reviews/2008-08-wag-the-dog?q=Jane+Rosenthal [Accessed 1 May 2013]

Habermas, Jürgen. *The Philosophical Discourse of Modernity: Twelve Lectures (Studies in Contemporary German Social Thought)*. Cambridge, MA: MIT Press, 1993.

Hammond, Mike. 'Media Event'. In Roberta Pearson and Philip Simpson (eds), *Critical Dictionary of Film and Television Theory*, 272–3. London and New York: Routledge, 2001.

Hansen, Miriam Bratu. *Cinema and Experience: Siegfried Kracauer, Walter Benjamin, and Theodor W. Adorno*. Berkeley: University of California Press, 2012.

Harris, John F. 'In The Midst of Scandal, Clinton Planned Action'. *Washington Post*, August 21, 1998, A1.

Hayden, Joseph. *Covering Clinton: The President and the Press in the 1990s*. Westport, CT: Praeger, 2002.

Healy, Gene. *The Cult of the Presidency: America's dangerous devotion to executive power*. Washington, DC: Cato Institute, 2008.

Herbert, Bob. 'In America; What to think?' *New York Times*, 17 December 1998.

Hersh, Seymour M. 'Annals of National Security, The Missiles of August'. *The New Yorker*, 12 October 1998.

Hertsgaard, Mark. *On Bended Knee: The Press and The Reagan Presidency*. New York: Schocken Books, 1989.

Hilliard, Robert L. *Hollywood Speaks Out: Pictures that Dared to Protest Real World Issues*. Malden, MA: Wiley-Blackwell, 2009.

Hitchens, Christopher. 'Most Dangerous Presidency: weapons of mass distraction'. *Vanity Fair*, March 1999.

Hoskins, Andrew. 'Constructing History in TV News from Clinton to 9/11: Flashframes of History-American Visual Memories'. In David Holloway and John Beck (eds), *American Visual Cultures*, 299–305. New York: Continuum Publishing, 2005.

Hunter, Stephen. 'A Tale that Wags the Dog'. *Washington Post*, 26 January 1998.

Hüppauf, Bernd. 'Experiences of Modern Warfare and the Crisis of Representation'. *New German Critique* 59 (1993): 41–77.

'Is it life or is it Mamet?' *Economist*, 29 January 1998. http://www.economist.com/node/112045 [Accessed 1 May 2013]

Jakobson, Roman. 'Closing statements: Linguistics and Poetics'. In T. A. Sebeok ed, *Style in language*. Cambridge, MA: MIT Press, 1960.

Jaramillo, Deborah L. *Ugly War, Pretty Package: How CNN and Fox News Made the Invasion of Iraq High Concept*. Bloomington: Indiana University Press, 2009.

Jenkins, Henry and David Thorburn. 'Introduction: Toward an Aesthetics of Transition'. In Henry Jenkins and David Thorburn(eds), *Rethinking Media Change: The Aesthetics of Transition*, 1–16. Cambridge, MA: MIT Press, 2003.

Jenkins, Keith. *Images of Terror: What We Can and Can't Know about Terrorism*. New York: Aldine de Gruyter, 2003.

Johnson, Gary. 'Wag the dog'. *Images: A Journal of Film and Popular Culture*, Issue 5, (1998). http://www.imagesjournal.com/issue05/reviews/wag.htm [Accessed 1 May 2013]

Kauffmann, Sylvie. 'Un répit bienvenu pour un président malmené'. *Monde*, 22 February 1998.

Kellner, Douglas. *Media Culture*. London and New York: Routledge, 1995.

—*Cinema Wars: Hollywood Film and Politics in the Bush-Cheney Era*. Malden, MA: Wiley-Blackwell, 2010.

Keyishian, Harry. *Screening Politics; The Politician in American Movies, 1931–2001*. Lanham, Maryland: Scarecrow Press, 2003.

Kitses, Jim. *Horizons West: Anthony Mann, Budd Boetticher, Sam Peckinpah: Studies of Authorship Within the Western*. London: Thames and Hudson, 1969.

Kittler, Friedrich. 'Fiktion und Simulation'. In Ars Electronica ed, *Philosophien der neuen Technologie*, 57–80. Berlin: Merve Publishers, 1989.

—*Optical Media*. Cambridge: Polity Press, 2010.
Koch, Gertrude. *Siegfried Kracauer: An Introduction*. Princeton, NJ: Princeton University Press, 2000.
Kracauer, Siegfried. *Theory of Film: The Redemption of Physical Reality*. Princeton, NJ: Princeton University Press, 1997.
—*Siegfried Kracauer's American Writings: Essays on Film and Popular Culture*. Johannes von Moltke and Kristy Rawson (eds). Berkeley: University of California Press, 2012.
Kurtz, Howard. 'The day the stories snowballed'. *Washington Post*, 17 December 1998.
Latour, Bruno. *Science in Action: How to Follow Scientists and Engineers Through Society*. Cambridge, Massachusetts: Harvard University Press, 1987.
—*Re-assembling the social: An Introduction to Actor-Network-Theory*. New York: Oxford University Press, 2005.
Lefebvre, Martin and Marc Furstenau. 'Digital editing and montage: the vanishing celluloid and beyond'. *CiNéMAS* 13, 1–2 (2002): 69–107.
LeGrice, Malcolm. *Experimental Cinema in the Digital Age*. London: BFI, 2001.
Levin, Thomas. 'Rhetoric of the Temporal Index: Surveillant Narration and the Cinema of "Real Time"'. In Thomas Levin, Ursula Frohne, and Peter Weibel (eds), *CTRL Space: Rhetorics of Surveillance from Bentham to Big Brother*, 578–93. Karlsruhe: Center for Art and Media, 2002.
Levinson, Barry. 'Hey, we were just kidding'. *Newsweek U.S. Edition*, 9 February 1998. http://newsweek.com/nw-srv/issue/06_98a/nw_980209_051_1.htm [Accessed 15 March 1999].
Levy, Emanuel *Cinema of Outsiders: The Rise of American Independent Film*. New York and London: New York University Press, 1999.
Lezotte, Suzanne. 'Phedon Papamichael, ASC, Lenses "The Ides of March"'. *Panavision*, 7 October 2011. http://www.panavision.com/spotlight/phedon-papamichael-asc-lenses-ides-march [Accessed 1 May 2013]
Luhmann, Niklas. *The Reality of the Mass Media*. Stanford: Stanford University Press, 2000.
MacCabe, Bob. 'Barthes and Bazin: The Ontology of the Image'. In Jean-Michel Rabaté ed. *Writing the Image after Roland Barthes*, 71–6. Philadelphia: University of Pennsylvania Press, 1997.
—'Wag the dog'. *Empire* 106 (1998). http://www.empireonline.com/site/incinemas/ReviewInFull.asp?FID=3552 [Accessed 30 May 1999]
Maltby, Richard. *Hollywood Cinema*. Malden, MA: Blackwell Publishing, 2003.
Manheim, Jarol. 'Strategic Public Diplomacy: Managing Kuwait's Image During the Gulf Conflict'. In W. Lance Bennett and David L. Paletz (eds), *Taken by storm: the media, public opinion, and U.S. foreign policy in the Gulf War*, 131–48. Chicago: University of Chicago Press, 1994.

Manovich, Lev. *The Language of New Media*. Cambridge, MA: MIT Press, 2001.

Martin, Andy, Dan Franc and Daniela Zounkova. *Outdoor and Experiential Learning: An Holistic and Creative Approach to Programme Design*. New York: Gower, 2004.

Maslin, Janet. 'At Sundance, Talk Of Life Imitating Art'. *New York Times*, 24 January 1998. http://www.nytimes.com/1998/01/24/movies/critic-s-notebook-at-sundance-talk-of-life-imitating-art.html?pagewanted=all [Accessed 10 January 2012]\.

Mason, Carol. 'The Hillbilly defense: culturally mediating US terror at home and abroad'. *NWSA Journal*, 17, 3 (2005): 39–63.

Mitchell, William J. *The Reconfigured Eye. Visual Truth in the Post-Photographic Era*. Cambridge, MA: MIT Press, 1992.

Morrow, Lance. 'The Reckless and the Stupid'. *Time Magazine*, 151, 4, 2 February 1998. http://www.time.com/time/magazine/article/0,9171,987761,00.html [Accessed 1 May 2013]

Mulard, Claudine. 'L' actualité américaine rattrape les films Wag the Dog et Primary Colors'. *Monde*, 21 February 1998.

Murray, Timothy. 'By way of introduction: digitality and the memory of cinema, or, bearing the losses of the digital code'. *Wide Angle* 21, 1 (1999): 3–24.

Neale, Steve. 'Questions of genre'. In Barry Keith Grant ed. *Film Genre Reader II*, 157–83. Texas: University Texas Press, 1995.

—*Genre and Hollywood*. London and New York: Routledge, 2000.

Neve, Brian. *Film and Politics in America: A Social Tradition*. London: Routledge, 1992.

—'Frames of presidential and candidate politics in American films of the 1990s'. *The Public* Vol. 7 (2000): 19–32.

Nichols, Bill. *Representing Reality: issues and concepts in documentary*. Bloomington: Indiana University Press, 1991.

—*Blurred Boundaries: Questions of Meaning in Contemporary Culture*. Bloomington and Indianapolis: Indiana University Press, 1994.

Parry-Giles, J. and Parry-Giles T. 'Meta-Imaging, The War Room, and the Hyperreality of U.S. Politics'. *Journal of Communication* 49 (1999): 28–45.

Plantinga, Carl. 'Moving Pictures and the Rhetoric of Nonfiction Film: Two Approaches'. In David Bordwell and Noël Carroll (eds), *Post-Theory: Reconstructing Film Studies*, 307–24. Madison: University of Wisconsin Press, 1996.

Price, S. L. 'Much Ado About Nothing'. *Vanity Fair*, March 2012. http://www.vanityfair.com/hollywood/2012/03/diner-201203 [Accessed 1 May 2013]

Quart, Leonard and Albert Auster. *American Film and Society since 1945: Third Edition, Revised and Expanded*. Westport, Connecticut: Praeger, 2001.

Rabinow, Paul. *The Foucault reader*. London: Penguin Books, 1991.

Renov, Michael. *Theorizing Documentary*. New York: Routledge, 1993.

Rezun, Miron. *Europe's Nightmare: the Struggle for Kosovo*. Westport, CT: Praeger, 2001.

Rollins, Peter and John O'Connor. *Hollywood's White House: The American Presidency in Film and History*. Lexington, KY: University Press of Kentucky, 2003.

Rollins, Peter. 'Hollywood's Presidents, 1944–1996: The Primacy of Character'. In Peter C. Rollins and John E. Connor (eds), *Hollywood's White House: The American Presidency in Film and History*, 251–62. Lexington, KY: Kentucky University Press, 2003.

Rosen, Philip. *Change Mummified: Cinema, Historicity, Theory*. Minneapolis: Minnesota University Press, 2001.

Rosenstone, Robert. *History on film/film on history*. New York: Longman/Pearson, 2006.

Rothman, William. 'The Filmmaker as Hunter: Robert Flaherty's *Nanook of the North*'. In Barry Keith Grant and Jeannette Sloniowski (eds), *Documenting the Documentary: close readings of documentary film and video*, 23–39. Detroit: Wayne State University Press, 1998.

Rowe, John Carlos. 'Culture, US Imperialism, and Globalization'. *American Literary History* 16, 4 (2004): 575–95.

—ed. *A Concise Companion to American Studies*. New York: Wiley-Blackwell, 2010.

Santaella-Braga, Lucia. 'The prephotographic, the photographic, and the postphotographic image'. In Winfried Nöth ed. *Semiotics of the Media. State of the Art, Projects, and Perspectives*, 121–32. Berlin and New York: Mouton de Gruyter, 1997.

Sarris, Andrew. *Politics and Cinema*. New York: Columbia University Press, 1978.

Scarry, Elaine. 'Watching and Authorizing the Gulf War'. In Marjorie Garber, John Matlock, and Rebecca L. Walkowitz (eds), *Media Spectacles*, 57–73. New York, London: Routledge, 1993.

Schmidt, Susan, Peter Baker, and Toni Locy. 'Clinton Accused of Urging Aide to Lie'. *The Washington Post*, 21 January 1998. http://www.washingtonpost.com/wp-srv/politics/special/clinton/stories/clinton012198.htm [Accessed 26 August 2010].

Scott, Ian. *American Politics in Hollywood Film*. Edinburgh: Edinburgh University Press], 2000.

Shales, Tom. *Washington Post,* 21 August, 1998, B01.

Shaw, David. 'Dire Judgement on Clinton Started Just Days into Term'. *Los Angeles Times*, 16 September 1993. http://articles.latimes.com/1993-09-16/news/mn-35815_1_clinton-presidency [Accessed 14 April 2011].

Schmitt, Rudolf, 'Systematic Metaphor Analysis as a Method of Qualitative Research'. *The Qualitative Report* 10, 2 (2005): 358–94.

'So true to life you may have seen the media first'. *Sunday Times*, 24 May 1998. www.suntimes.co.za/1998/05/24/arts/ane11.htm [Accessed 24 December 2004]

Souriau, Etienne. 'La structure de l'univers filmique et le vocabulaire de la filmologie'. *Revue Internationale de Filmologie* 7–8 (1951): 231–40.

Spielmann, Yvonne. 'Aesthetic features in digital imaging: collage and morph'. *Wide Angle* 21, 1 (1999): 131–48.

Stam, Robert, Robert Burgoyne, and Sandy Flitterman-Lewis. *New Vocabularies in*

Film Semiotics: Structuralism, Poststructuralism and Beyond. London, New York: Routledge, 1993.

Stauber, John and Sheldon Rampton. *Toxic sludge is good for you: lies, damn lies, and the public relations industry*. Monroe, ME: Common Courage Press, 1995.

Stempel, Tom. 'The Collaborative Dog: *Wag the Dog* (1997)' *Film & History: An Interdisciplinary Journal of Film and Television Studies* 35, 1 (2005): 60–4.

Tatara, Paul. '"Wag the Dog" grabs satire by the tail.' *CNN*, 6 January 1998. http://edition.cnn.com/SHOWBIZ/9801/06/wag.dog.review/ [Accessed 1 May 2013]

Taylor, Philip, P. *War and the Media: Propaganda and Persuasion in the Gulf War*. Manchester: Manchester University Press, 1992.

Thanouli, Eleftheria. *Post-Classical Cinema: An International Poetics of Film Narration*. London: Wallflower Press, 2009.

Thompson, Daniel. *Levinson on Levinson*. London: Faber & Faber, 1992.

Tredell, Nicolas ed. *Cinemas of the Mind*. Cambridge: Icon Books, 2002.

Turan, Kenneth. 'Wag the Dog Is a Comedy With Some Real Bite to It.' *Los Angeles Times*, 24 December 1997. http://articles.latimes.com/1997/dec/24/entertainment/ca-1649 [Accessed 1 May 2013]

Turim, Maureen. 'Artisanal prefigurations of the digital: animating realities, collage effects, and theories of image manipulation.' *Wide Angle* 21, 1 (1999): 49–62.

Uricchio, William. 'Historicizing media in transition.' In David Thorburn and Henry Jenkins (eds), *Rethinking Media Change: The Aesthetics of Transition*, 23–38. Cambridge, MA: MIT Press, 2003.

Vance, Eugene. 'The Past as Text and the Historiography of Tomorrow: Notes on a Recent Book.' *MLN* 113, 4 (1998): 951–79.

'*Wag the Dog* back in spotlight.' *CNN*, 21 August 1998. http://edition.cnn.com/ALLPOLITICS/1998/08/21/wag.the.dog/ [Accessed 1 May 2013]

Walton, Jennifer Lee. *A Rhetorical Analysis of Six Hollywood films about Politics: Presenting the Candidate as a Movie Star*. New York: Edwin Mellen Press, 2008.

Weber, Cynthia. *International Relations Theory: A Critical Introduction*. New York: Routledge, 2001.

Wicks, Robert. *Understanding Audiences:* Learning To Use the Media Constructively. New York: Routledge, 2001.

Wright, Will. *Sixguns & Society: A Structural Study of the Western*. Berkeley: University of California Press, 1975.

Wyatt, Justin. *High Concept: Movies and Marketing in Hollywood*. Austin: University of Texas Press, 1994.

Index

ABC cover up 79
Actor-Network Theory 123
Advise and Consent (1962) 125
Afghanistan 91
afilmic reality 17, 21, 143-4, 146 *see also* Souriau, Etienne
agency 10, 25-6, 126, 137-8
   and *Avalon* (1990) 37-8
   and *Candidate, The* (1972) 127-9
   human 32, 55, 114-20
   and *Ides of March, The* (2011) 133-5
   and *Man of the Year* (2006) 40
   objects as 30-2, 44, 121-4
   and *Parallax View, The* (1974) 129-30
   and *Primary Colors* (1998) 131-3
   and *Wag the Dog* (1997) 26-7, 30, 32, 71, 106, 113-24
   and *War Room, The* (1993) 135-7
Air Force One (1997) 126
Al Shifa pharmaceutical plant 91
All the Kings Men (2006) 126
All the President's Men (1976) 112, 125
Allen, Woody 22
   Purple Rose of Cairo, The (1985) 10
   Zelig (1983) 19-20, 22
Altman, Rick 107, 109, 112
American exceptionalism 120
American Hero (Beinhart) 6
American President, The (1995) 126
analogue cinema 53, 60-1, 70
   and motion blur 63
Andrew, Dudley 5, 62, 146-7
animation 53-4
Ansen, David 88
Arnheim, Rudolf 2-3, 51
Assassination of Richard Nixon, The (2004) 126
astroturfing 97
Atwater, Lee 6
autopoetic system 123
Avalon (1990) 34, 36-8

Baker, James 6
Balász, Béla
   Spirit of Film, The 5
   Visible Man 5
Barthes, Roland 55
Baudrillard, Jean 58-9
Baum, Mattew 90-1
Bazin, André 2-4, 51-2, 55, 61, 62
   What is Cinema? 3, 51
Beinhart, Larry 6
Belushi, James 32, 96
Best Man, The (1964) 125
Bob Roberts (1991) 113
Bolter, Jay David 63, 69
Bordwell, David 19, 24, 25
Branigan, Edward 20-2, 24, 33, 44, 147
   narrative theory 24-6, 30
   Narrative Comprehension and Film 20, 24
Buckland, Warren 63
Bulworth (1998) 117, 126
Bush, George H. W. 6, 79, 82
Bush, George W. 117
Bush administration, the 79-82, 94

Candidate, The (1972) 113, 117, 127-9, 130, 137
Carroll, Noel 19, 22
CGI 56-7 *see also* special effects
Christensen, Terry 108-9, 130
   Reel Politics 108
cinema/reality binary 7-8, 17-23 *see also* Souriau, Etienne; fiction/non-fiction dichotomy
   and technology 53-4, 149-50
   and *Wag the Dog* (1997) 57-8, 77-8, 86-93, 97-9
   and *War Room, The* (1993) 135-7
Clinton, Bill 1, 7, 33, 131
   and Lewinsky scandal 7, 86-92, 134

and military action 7, 87, 89–92, 149
and press manipulation 83–4
promiscuous behaviour of 83–4
and *War Room, The* (1993) 135–7
Clooney, George 133
Cohen, William 90
commodification 95–7
communication policy 82–3
Constructing the Political Spectacle (Edelman) 84
Coyne, Michael 107–8, 113,
and taxonomy of film 124–6, 127, 131, 133
Washington Goes to Hollywood (2008) 107, 124
creatorial level 18, 148
cultural verisimilitude 10, 64, 110–13, 128, 131

Dave (1993) 126
De Nero, Robert 28, 77
Desert Fox operation 91–2 *see also* Iraq
diegesis 18, 27–30, 145–7 *see also* Souriau, Etienne
digital cinema 4, 51–7, 60–1, 70, 98–9
and motion blur 63
and special effects 63
'Digital editing and montage: the vanishing celluloid and beyond' (Lefebvre and Furstenau) 56
Diner (1982) 33–5, 148
Dixon, Wheeler Winston 55
documentaries 19, 23, 61 *see also* non-fiction
Douchet, Jean 55, 61

Edelman, Murray 84–5
Constructing the Political Spectacle 84
Eisenstein, Sergei 2–4, 51–2
Elsaesser, Thomas 4–5, 27, 61, 99
Film Theory: An Introduction Through the Senses 4–5
'Louis Lumière – the cinema's first virtualist' 61
'and pathos of failure' 114

and realism 62
Executive Action (1973) 125

FAIR (Fairness and Accuracy in Reporting) 80, 81
fiction 18–23, 29–30, 42–4, 53, 56, 93
fiction/non-fiction dichotomy 18–23, 43
see also cinema/reality bipolar; fiction; high-concept filmmaking *and* non-fiction
and *Man of the Year* (2006) 39
and the media 99
and *Poliwood* (2009) 41–2
and *Wag The Dog* (1997) 29–30, 33, 43–4, 49, 71, 147–8
Film Theory: An Introduction Through the Senses (Elsaesser and Hagener) 4–5
filmic universe, the 17–18, 56, 143–8 *see also* Souriau Etienne
filmographic reality 17, 144–5, 146 *see also* Souriau, Etienne
filmology 17, 143
filmophanic reality 17–18, 145 *see also* Souriau, Etienne
Flaherty, Robert J.
Nanook of the North (1922) 61
Forrest Gump (1994) 63
Foucault, Michel 67, 98, 137
Frankenheimer, John 125
Furstenau, Marc 56

Gabriel over the White House (1930) 125
Gaylard, Gerard 69
generic verisimilitude 64, 111
genre 107–11, 137
Genre and Hollywood (Neale) 107
Gergen, David 78, 82, 84
Good Night and Good Luck (2005) 112, 126
Grusin, Richard 63
Gulf War (1991) 6, 58–59, 78–82, 98, 143 *see also* Iraq
and declaration of war 80–1
and dissident views 80
and Fairness and Accuracy in Reporting (FAIR) 80

and propaganda 79–81
role of television in 79–82, 123–4

Hagener, Malte 4–5
Film Theory: An Introduction Through the Senses 4–5
Hegedus, Chris 135, 137
Henkin, Hilary 6–7, 88
hero, the 84–6, 96, 114, 117–18
Hersh, Seymour 91
high-concept filmmaking 93–6, 98, 144, 151n. 1
high-concept war coverage 93–6, 98
Hill & Knowlton 79–80
Hitler, Adolf 80
Hoffman, Dustin 27, 77, 88
Hollywood
   and agency 114
   cinema 62, 93, 109–15
   connection with Washington 88, 99, 112–13
   and US politics 124–5 *see also* political films
   and World War II 149–50
Hussein, Saddam 80, 94

Ides of March, The (2011) 133–5
image, the 3, 56–8, 70, 128
immediacy 63–7, 69, 146–7
In the Line of Fire (1993) 125
Independence Day (1996) 126
indexing 22–3, 43
Industrial Light and Magic 63
intertextuality 94
Intolerance (1916) 107
Iraq 89 *see also* Gulf War
   bombing of 87, 89, 91–2
   and invasion of Kuwait/Saudia Arabia 79–80
   2003 invasion of 94–5
   and *Wag the Dog* (1997) 92
Iwo Jima photograph 58

Jaramillo, Deborah 93–5
JFK (1991) 125

Kennedy, John F. 83, 125
Khaldai, Yevgney 58

Klein, Joe 131
Kracauer, Siegfried 2–3, 5, 52
Theory of Film 3
Kuwait 79–80

Language of New Media, The (Manovich) 53
Larner, Jeremy 113
Latour, Bruno 123
Reassembling the Social 123
Lefebvre, Martin 56
Levin, Thomas 65
   'Rhetoric of the temporal index: surveillance narration and the cinema of "real time"' 65
Levinson, Barry 6–7 *see also Wag the Dog* (1997)
   and agency 16, 138
   appearance in *Wag the Dog* (1997) 29–30, 44, 49
   Avalon (1990) 34, 36–8
   Diner (1982) 33–5
   Levinson on Levinson 33–4
   and Lewinsky scandal 88
   Man of the Year (2006) 39–41, 109–10
   Poliwood (2009) 41–2
   shooting style 29, 31–2, 34–6, 39–40, 42
   Sphere (1998) 6
   and television, role of 33–8, 40–2, 44, 148 *see also* role of media in *under* *Wag the Dog* (1997)
Levinson on Levinson (Levinson) 33–4
Lewinsky, Monica 1, 7, 86–7
Lewinsky scandal 1, 7, 10, 32–3, 86–91, 134
   press reaction to 88–91
Los Angeles Times 88
'Louis Lumière – the cinema's first virtualist' (Elsaesser) 61
Lucas, George 34
Luhmann, Niklas 123–4
Lumière, Louis 61
Lynch, Jessica 95

Mamet, David 6–7, 88–9
Man of the Year (2006) 39–41, 109–10

Manchurian Candidate, The (1962) 125
Manchurian Candidate, The (2004) 126
Manovich, Lev 53–4
  Language of New Media, The 53
media, the 15, 149 *see also* immediacy; remediation; spin doctoring
  in *Candidate, The* (1972) 127–9
  and Clinton, Bill 89–92
  and the Gulf War 79–82
  and Levinson, Barry 33–42
  and North, Oliver 85–6
  and 2003 invasion of Iraq 94–5
  and *Wag the Dog* (1997) 78, 87–92, 98–9
  in *Wag the Dog* (1997) 30–3, 59, 68, 96–7, 121–4, 145–6
media event 78, 100n. 5
mediation 44, 144
'meta-imaging' 137
Monde, Le 87–8, 89–90
montage 4
Mr Smith Goes to Washington (1939) 117, 125
Murray, Forrest 113

Nanook of the North (1922) 61
Narrative Comprehension and Film (Branigan) 20, 24
narrative theory 24–6
narratives 19, 114
national hero, the 85–6, 96 *see also* hero, the; war narrative
national security 84–5
Nayirah 80
Neale, Steve 64, 107–8, 110
  Genre and Hollywood 107
  'Questions of genre' 108
New York Times 87, 90, 92
New Yorker 91
newspapers 87–90, 91–2 *see also* media, the; press, the
Newsweek 88
Niccol, Andrew 55
Nichols, Bill 19, 61
Nichols, Mike 131
Night and Fog (1955) 23
Nixon, Richard 82, 117
non-fiction 18–23, 61

North, Oliver 78, 85–6

Obama, Barack 78, 92, 135

Pakula, Alan 129
Papamichail, Phedon 133
paradoxes (in American history) 108
Parallax View, The (1974) 125, 129–30, 133
'pathos of failure' 114
Pennebaker, D. A. 135, 137
'performative agent' 117 *see also* agency; hero, the
photography 3, 53–6, 58
Plantinga, Carl 61
'Political Film in the Nineties' (Prince) 107
political films 105–13, 124–7, 137–8 *see also Wag the Dog* (1997)
  The Candidate, The (1972) 113, 127–9
  Ides of March, The 133–5
  Parallax View, The (1974) 125, 129–30
  Primary Colors (1998) 131–3
  taxonomy of 124–6
  War Room, The (1993) 135–7
political power 59
politics 84 *see also* political films
  and celebrity 41
  and image 128
  and *Wag the Dog* (1997) 7, 92, 98, 113–20
Poliwood (2009) 16, 41–2
press, the 82–4, 87–92 *see also* media, the; newspapers; spin doctoring
press manipulation *see* spin doctoring
Primary Colors (1998) 131–3
Prince, Stephen 107
  'Political Film in the Nineties' 107
profilmic reality 17, 144, 146 *see also* Souriau, Etienne
propaganda 59, 79–81 *see also* spin doctoring
public relations campaigns 79–82, 97, 122–3, 128 *see also* spin doctoring
Purple Rose of Cairo, The (1985) 10

'Questions of genre' (Neale) 108

Reagan, Ronald 82–3, 125
realism 10, 51, 55, 62–70 *see also* cultural verisimilitude
reality and fiction 87–9, 136–7 *see also* cinema/reality bipolar
Reel Politics (Christensen) 108
regime of truth 10, 67–9
remediation 63
Resnais, Alan 23
   Night and Fog (1955) 23
Revue Internationale de Filmologie 17
'Rhetoric of the temporal index: surveillance narration and the cinema of "real time"' (Levin) 65
Ritchie, Michael 127–8
Rosenthal, Joe 58

Saving Jessica Lynch (2003) 95
Schindler's List (1993) 23
Schlesinger, Arthur M., Jr. 108
Seconds (1966) 125
Seven Days in May (1964) 125
Simone (2002) 55
simulation 58–60
'sliding signifier' 27
sound 51–2
Souriau, Etienne 17–18, 56, 143–6
   'Structure of the Filmic Universe and the Vocabulary of Filmology, The' 17
special effects 54, 60, 63 *see also* CGI
spectatorial events 18, 147–8
Spielberg, Steven 23, 34
   Schindler's List (1993) 23
spin doctoring 82–4, 122 *see also* propaganda; role of media in *under Wag the Dog* (1997)
Spirit of Film, The (Balász) 5
'Structure of the Filmic Universe and the Vocabulary of Filmology, The' (Souriau) 17
Sudan 87, 91
surveillance 64–5

television, role of *see also* media, the
   and Gulf War (1991) 79–82
   and Levinson, Barry 33–42, 44, 148
   news 90–1, 94–5
   and propaganda 79
   and 2003 invasion of Iraq 94–5
   and *Wag the Dog* (1997) 90–1
   in *Wag the Dog* (1997) 30–2, 44, 65–9, 121–3, 144
'The Reckless and the Stupid' 89
Theory of Film (Kracauer) 3
Time 89
Tribeca 6
Turan, Kenneth 88
24 Hour Party People (2002) 20

Visible Man (Balász) 5

'Wag the Clinton' 89
Wag the Dog (1997) 126 *see also* Levinson, Barry
   and actor-network theory 123
   and agency 26–7, 30, 32, 71, 106, 113–24
   Albanian war 15–16, 49–50, 64, 68–9, 96–7, 118
   Brean (character) 57–8, 68–9, 119–20
   and cinema/reality binary 57–8, 77–8, 86–93, 97–9
   and digital technology 49–50, 60–1, 70–1
   and fiction/non-fiction dichotomy 29–30, 33, 43–4, 49, 71, 147–8
   heroes in 117–19
   human agency in 113–20
   and Iraq 92
   and media, the 78, 87–92, 98–9
   as media event 78
   Motss (character) 117–19
   music in 96–7
   narrative mode of 24, 26–33, 43–4
   non-fictional reading of 33
   objects as agents in 121–4
   plot of 15–16
   political context 86–92
   in political culture 92
   politicians in 116–17
   and politics 7, 92, 98, 113–20
   the President in 115–16
   reading of 33
   and reality 57–62, 86–91
   release of 77–8

  reviews of 87–8
  role of the media in 30–3, 59, 68, 96–7, 121–4, 145–6
  role of television in 30–2, 44, 65–9, 121–3, 144
  shooting style in 29, 31–2, 49–50, 128
  and Souriau's filmic universe 143–8
  and television 90–1
  title of 26
war films 112
war imagery 57–8
war narrative 94–6 *see also* national hero
War Room, The (1993) 135–7

Washington, DC 88, 99–100 *see also* political films
Washington Goes to Hollywood (Coyne) 107, 124
Washington Post 77, 87, 89, 90
What is Cinema? (Bazin) 3, 51
Wilde, Oscar 1
Willis, Gordon 133
Winterbottom, Michael 20
  24 Hour Party People (2002) 20
Wyatt, Justin 93, 95

Zelig (1983) 19–20, 22

www.ingramcontent.com/pod-product-compliance
Lightning Source LLC
Chambersburg PA
CBHW061838300426
44115CB00013B/2435